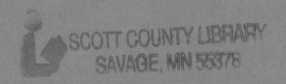

Glue & Go Costumes for Kids

Glue & Go Costumes for Kids

Super-Duper Designs with Everyday Materials

Holly Cleeland

photographs by Larry Lytle

Sterling Publishing Co., Inc.
New York

illustrations by Colin Hayes
edited by Isabel Stein
designed by Wanda Kossak

Library of Congress Cataloging-in-Publication Data

Cleeland, Holly.
  Glue & go costumes for kids : super-duper designs with everyday
materials / Holly Cleeland ; photographs by Larry Lytle.
      p. cm.
    Includes index.
    ISBN 0-8069-9283-2
    1. Children's costumes. I. Title: Glue and go costumes for kids. II.
Title.
TT633 .C58 2004
646.4'78–dc22

2003024266

10 9 8 7 6 5 4 3 2

Published by Sterling Publishing Co., Inc.
387 Park Avenue South, New York, NY 10016
© 2004 by Holly Cleeland
Distributed in Canada by Sterling Publishing
c/o Canadian Manda Group, 165 Dufferin Street
Toronto, Ontario, Canada M6K 3H6
Distributed in Great Britain and Europe by Chris Lloyd at Orca
Book Services, Stanley House, Fleets Lane, Poole BH15 3AJ, England
Distributed in Australia by Capricorn Link (Australia) Pty. Ltd.
P.O. Box 704, Windsor, NSW 2756, Australia

Sterling ISBN 0-8069-9283-2

Contents

Introduction

Ready for a creative adventure? Plug in the hot glue gun, grab the packing tape, clean out the plastic cups, and prepare to build fabulous memories with lots of laughs along the way.

Costume-making means a lot to me because I was the child who wanted to win the costume contest. I was tired of being the child that circled the costume parade as people scratched their heads every time I passed by, not knowing what I was.

As I grew older, I created costumes for kids in the neighborhood. During one contest, my neighborhood friend circled around in the costume parade as people pointed and stared at the costume I made. It was delightful to see my friend's face when he realized he stood out as the winner. The smile on his face grew bigger and brighter with each lap that he made. For that moment in time he was outstanding. A memory was created that would last a lifetime.

Several costume contests and lots of happy memories later, I bring the fun to you. I hope that you too will enjoy stimulating your creative imagination, broadening your reach as an artist, and developing memories with family and friends as you build prize-winning costumes together.

Before You Start

Building costumes can be a lot of fun. When there are young children around, there are a few do's and don'ts to keep in mind. Do keep all sharp tools, pins, hot glue guns, power tools, etc., out of the reach of very young children. For the parts of the projects that demand your focused attention, such as cutting foam core board, try to find a time when you aren't distracted by small persons asking for apple juice or jumping off chairs. Read through a project entirely before you get started and be sure you have all the tools and supplies that you need on hand. Protect your work surface with a few layers of scrap cardboard when you are cutting. Work in a place with good ventilation when you are using materials whose vapors or dust could be irritating.

To enlarge patterns, reproduce the grid given in the book with light pencil lines on the foam core or cardboard, making the boxes the size indicated on each grid. Then redraw the enlarged pattern on the cardboard or foam core board, using the small pattern as a guide, working box by box.

While you work on the costume, very young children can help by making collages of wrapping paper or crepe paper decorations for a party area. They can make drawings of costumes they'd like to see, cut out pictures of dressed-up people from an old magazine, or make an accompanying paper costume for a favorite doll or bear. Older children can help with measuring and enlarging patterns, painting costumes, taping and gluing, and cutting paper and other things, as long as they are closely supervised. You know best what your children can do. Don't expect perfection from yourself or from them, but share the fun of creating something together.

If children will be walking around in their costumes in the dark, add some reflective tape so they can be seen easily. If a child is wearing a costume that cuts off the child's vision, plan to accompany the child as he or she walks around. (You probably would want to do this anyway.) Be sure children won't be near open flames in flammable costumes. For a party, plan the clothes underneath the costume so the child will still look festive if he or she takes off the large parts of the costume.

Where to Find Materials

You'll probably find a wealth of materials you can use for costumes. Here are some places to look:

- acrylic paint: art supply store or craft store
- cardboard tubes: center core of wrapping paper or paper towels
- clear packing tape: office supply or shipping store
- colored tape: hardware store
- corrugated cardboard: art supply store; or use disassembled boxes (lay them flat and tape together in the shape that the costume requires)
- drywall screws: hardware store
- polyester batting: fabric store
- flexible polyurethane foam: craft store, upholstery store
- foam core board: art supply store
- polyurethane foam: foam store, mattress company
- Plastifoam™: craft supply store
- Plexiglas®: hardware store
- polyethylene tubing: hardware store, pet store
- PVC tubing and connectors: hardware store, craft store
- modeling clay: craft store
- ricrac: fabric store
- Mylar™ sheets: art supply store or sign shop
- star decorations, bows, bunting: party supply store
- Styrofoam® balls, eggs, cones: craft store

Artist's Palette

MATERIALS

- 33" × 48" (84 × 122 cm) white foam core board, ½" (1.5 cm) thick
- acrylic paint: red, orange, yellow, green, blue, purple, and hot pink
- seven 6" (15 cm) diameter balloons
- seven 12" × 12" (30.5 × 30.5 cm) pieces of white fabric
- 12 oz (360 mL) white glue
- 2 rolls of 1" (2.5 cm) wide white tape
- roll of 2" (5 cm) wide clear tape
- 3 black 12 oz (360 mL) plastic cups
- 36" (92 cm) strong white ribbon for strap, 1" (2.5 cm) wide
- 24" (61 cm) cardboard tube, 1½" (3.8 cm) wide
- 6" × 24" (15 × 61 cm) yellow wrapping paper
- Styrofoam coffee cup
- aluminum foil to wrap coffee cup
- newspaper

TOOLS: craft knife, paintbrush, scissors, large bowl, hot glue gun, pencil, ruler

CHILD WEARS: black clothes and red beret

DIRECTIONS

1 Draw the enlarged palette shape on foam core board and cut the palette shape out with a craft knife.

2 Tape over edges with 1" (2.5 cm) wide white tape for a clean line around palette and circle.

3 To make a strap for the costume, find the top center and poke two holes in the top edge of the palette, centered on the width, with a 12"

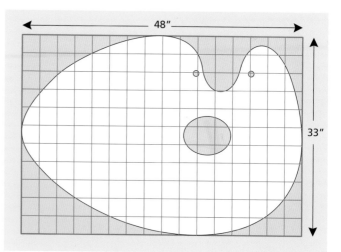

Step 1. Pattern for palette. 1 box = 3" (7.6 cm). Cut away blue parts. Dots indicate holes for straps.

(30.5 cm) gap between the holes (see pattern). Tie the white ribbon through the holes. Try it on the child and be sure it is the correct length. Tape down the ribbon ends with clear tape.

4 Protect work surface with newspaper or plastic. Take cap off of white glue and pour all of the glue into a large bowl. Fill the empty glue container with water (so you have an equal amount of water to glue), and stir all of the water into the glue until the glue is completely dissolved. Blow up balloons until they are 6" (15 cm) in diameter and tie off. Soak the white sheets of fabric in the glue mixture, one at a time, and wrap each balloon with one. Let dry overnight.

5 Once they are completely dry, use something sharp to pop the balloons, leaving the stiff outer shells of fabric. With your hands, scrunch and shape the shells so they look like paints on a palette. Paint these shells with the acrylic paints, a different color for each shell. When the paint is dry, hot-glue the shells to the palette.

6 Wrap the 24" (61 cm) cardboard tube with yellow wrapping paper.

7 Tape the Styrofoam coffee cup to one end of the cardboard tube, with the open end of the coffee cup facing out. Cover the cup all over outside and on its edge with aluminum foil. Together these will become the handle and ferrule for the paintbrush.

8 Take 3 black 12 oz (360 mL) plastic cups. Use scissors to make vertical cuts ½" (1.5 cm) apart from the rim of each cup to the base. These cups will be the bristles for the paintbrush.

9 Tape one black cup inside the cup covered in aluminum foil at the end of the paintbrush. Tape the second black cup inside the first black cup. Repeat with the last cup.

10 Tape the artist's brush to the palette so the brush extends about 12" (30.5 cm) above the top of the palette.

Paint me a rainbow.

Bacon and Eggs

MATERIALS

- 30" × 42" (76 × 107 cm) piece of foam core board, ½" (1.2 cm) thick
- two 2-quart (1.9 L) plastic bowls
- two 12" × 30" (30.5 × 76 cm) white sheets of polyurethane foam, 1" (2.5 cm) thick
- 6" × 30" (15 × 76 cm) strip of scrap cardboard
- 1" (2.5 cm) wide roll of white tape
- acrylic paint: yellow, red, tan, and white; 2.5 oz (75 mL) of each
- roll of 2" (5 cm) wide clear packing tape
- red baseball cap
- 5 yards (4.6 m) of thin (20 gauge) wire
- two 18" (45 cm) pieces of strong white ribbon for ties

TOOLS: craft knife, small cotton paint roller, scissors, paintbrush, pencil, marker

CHILD WEARS: white T-shirt, black pants, and black shoes

DIRECTIONS

1 Draw the shape of fried egg whites on the 30" × 42" (76 × 107 cm) foam core board and cut out the white shape (see pattern).

2 Place the 2 plastic bowls on the egg white shape (see photo). Trace around the bowls, and use a craft knife to cut out slightly smaller circles from the foam core board.

3 Tape around the outside edges of the foam core board with white tape.

4 Poke two small holes for straps in the top of the egg white (see pattern), with a 12" (30.5 cm)

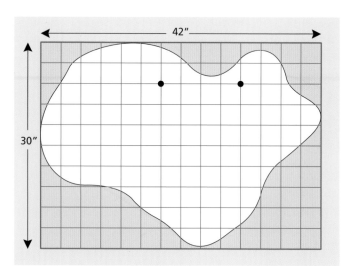

Step 1. Pattern for egg whites. 1 box = 3" (7.5 cm). Dots indicate holes for strap. Cut away blue parts.

gap between the holes. Tie an 18" (45 cm) piece of white ribbon through each of the holes and tape down the tied ends with clear tape. The ribbons are ties that will hold the costume on the child's neck.

5 Use the small cotton paint roller to cover the front of the foam core board with white acrylic paint. Let dry.

6 Mix a little red acrylic paint into your yellow paint to give it the orange tinge of an egg yolk and paint the undersides of the plastic bowls. Let dry.

7 Fit the bowls into the big holes in the egg white shape so that the rims are at the back and the rounded parts stick out the front, and tape to board from behind with the clear packing tape.

Start your morning off right!

8 Take the two sheets of polyurethane foam and use a marker to mark a wavy line on each long edge, like the edges of a strip of bacon (see photo for example). Cut on these lines with scissors.

9 To make a clean line while painting the foam strips to look like bacon, cut the 6" × 30" (15 × 76 cm) strip of cardboard so that it has a wavy line that roughly follows the edge of the foam. Then push the cardboard edge almost flush to the edge of the foam, leaving about 1" (2.5 cm) of the foam edge uncovered. Paint the uncovered foam edge with the red acrylic paint. Repeat this process on each side of each bacon strip. Paint a wavy red stripe down the middle of each piece to finish the bacon. Let dry.

10 Mix the tan paint with water. Make this very transparent. Lightly brush the foam bacon strips with this mixture to make the red paint and foam look tan. Let dry.

11 Run a piece of thin wire all around the edges of each foam bacon strip to help stiffen it, taking large running stitches with the wire along the edges as if it were thread. Twist wire ends together and cut off excess. Be sure to cover any wire ends with tape so they don't scratch anyone.

12 Poke two holes through the middle of each of the foam bacon strips with a short piece of wire. Take one of the bacon strips and wire it to the baseball cap in front (poke holes through the cap); it should balance well when the cap is on the child, and the child should be able to see easily when he is wearing the cap.

13 Wire one of the bacon strips to the bottom of the egg white shape by poking holes through the foam core and feeding the wire ends through to the back. Twist the wire's ends together to hold the bacon to the foam core, cutting off any excess. Tape down the wire ends so they won't stick the wearer.

Birdhouse

MATERIALS

- two 29" × 24" (73.5 × 61 cm) pieces of corrugated cardboard
- 24" × 40" (61 × 101.5 cm) piece of corrugated cardboard
- 24" × 24" (61 × 61 cm) piece of corrugated cardboard
- two 18" × 18" (45.5 × 45.5 cm) pieces of corrugated cardboard
- 28" × 36" (71 × 91.5 cm) yellow wrapping paper
- 28" × 72" (71 × 183 cm) green wrapping paper
- 24" × 72" (61 × 183 cm) white butcher paper
- 12" × 18" (30.5 × 45.5 cm) sheet of construction paper in each color: pink, purple, orange, yellow, red
- 12" × 12" (30.5 × 30.5 cm) sheet of blue construction paper (for bird in hair) or toy bird for hair ornament
- 12" (30.5 cm) cardboard tube, 1" (2.5 cm) wide
- lime green acrylic paint
- 2" (5 cm) wide roll clear packing tape
- white glue
- piece of newspaper
- bobby pin

TOOLS: scissors, craft knife, ¼" (5 mm) paintbrush, pencil, ruler, ruling compass

CHILD WEARS: black or white shirt, shoes in a neutral color

DIRECTIONS

1 Draw pattern and cut out the front and back of the birdhouse from the 29" × 24" (73.5 × 61 cm) cardboards.

2 Cut an 8" (20 cm) diameter circle out of the center of the front panel to create the door for the bird. Just below the door, cut out a 1" (2.5 cm) circle to hold the perch.

3 Tape an 18" × 18" (45.5 × 45.5 cm) side cardboard panel to the front panel, using clear tape, working from the bottom up; see diagram. Tape the back panel to the 18" × 18" side panel also. Tape the other 18" × 18" side panel to the other side of the front and back panels.

4 Once the cardboards are taped together, cover the front with yellow wrapping paper; tape the paper in place. Cover the sides with green wrapping paper; tape it in place.

5 Fold a 24" × 40" (61 × 101.5 cm) piece of cardboard in half so it is 24" × 20" (61 × 51 cm) to create the roof of the birdhouse. Flatten it out and wrap it with white butcher paper, taped in

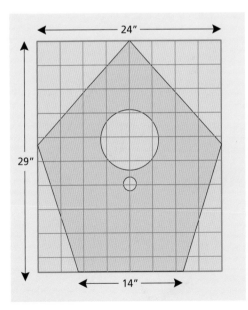

Steps 1 and 2. Pattern for front and back. 1 box = 3" (7.5 cm). Holes should be cut out only on front part. Cut away blue parts.

*Make a birdhouse
and see who
shows up!*

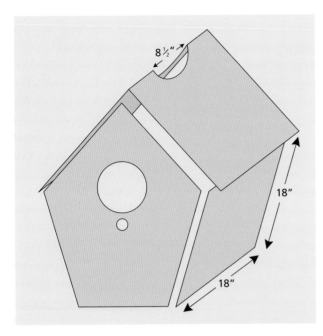

Step 3. Tape sides to front and back. Tape on roof in Step 5.

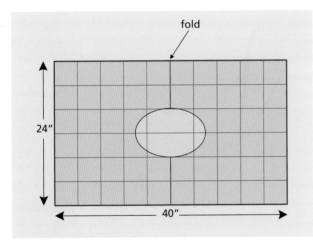

Step 5. Pattern for roof. 1 box = 4" (10 cm). Cut away oval.

place. Cut out an 8½" × 10" (21.5 × 25.5 cm) oval hole centered on the crease. The oval should extend about 5" (12.5 cm) on either side of the crease so that there will be room for the child's head once the roof has been folded and attached to the birdhouse. Try the roof on the child; enlarge oval if needed. Tape the roof to the top of the house, being sure the roof over-laps all around (see Step 3 diagram).

6 Stand the house on top of the 24" × 24" (61 × 61 cm) piece of cardboard (which will become the floor), leaving a 5" (12.5 cm) edge at the front. Trace a line around the base of the house onto the cardboard, and cut the house outline out of the cardboard floor with a craft knife to provide a space for the child to stand in inside the costume.

7 Cover the floor of the house with white paper, cutting away the paper over the inner space, and tape the floor with clear tape from inside the house to the sides of house. Glue a rolled-up newspaper to the front of the house (see photo).

8 Stack the 12" × 18" (30.5 × 45.5 cm) sheets of pink, purple, and red construction papers. On a separate piece of scratch paper or cardboard, draw a 3" (7.5 cm) flower shape and cut it out. Use that as a template to draw flower shapes with a pencil on the stacked construction paper. Cover the papers with as many flower shapes as can fit. Cut out the flowers, being careful to keep the stack of construction paper aligned, which keeps you from having to mark and cut each piece of construction paper sepa-rately.

9 Stack the 12" × 18" (30.5 × 45.5 cm) yellow and orange construction papers. Cover the top paper with 1" (2.5 cm) circles. Cut them out through all layers, being careful to keep the stack aligned.

10 Glue the pink, purple, and red flower shapes all over the roof and sides of birdhouse as seen in photo. Glue yellow and orange circles on top of flowers.

11 Insert and tape in the cardboard tube below the large hole to serve as bird perch.

12 Use the lime green paint and paintbrush to paint little stems and leaves around the flowers at the bottom of the birdhouse.

13 Fold a bird out of 12" × 12" (30.5 × 30.5 cm) blue construction paper, or use a toy bird for a hair decoration, bobby-pinning it in place.

Black Widow Spider

MATERIALS

- thirty-two 12 oz (360 mL) black plastic cups
- four 10" (25.5 cm) black plastic plates
- 10" (25.5 cm) red plastic plate
- four 1" (2.5 cm) wide × 24" (61 cm) black ribbons
- black baseball cap
- two black pipe cleaners
- ½" (1.2 cm) wide black tape
- 2" (5 cm) wide clear packing tape
- ¼" wide × 48" (0.5 × 122 cm) red ribbon for hair bows (optional)

TOOLS: scissors, ruler

CHILD WEARS: extra-large black sweatshirt, pillow, red tights, black shoes, red bows in hair

DIRECTIONS

1 With clear packing tape, tape together 4 black plastic plates into a diamond shape. On the upper black plate, cut 2 holes for straps, about 8" (20 cm) apart. Repeat this on the bottom of the diamond (the lower black plate). Tape the red plastic plate in the center of the diamond shape.

2 For a leg, tape 4 black plastic cups, one inside the next, in a stack, making a curved shape. Repeat this 7 times to make a total of 8 legs.

3 Tape 4 legs on the left side and 4 legs on the right side of the diamond shape with clear tape.

4 For straps, tie a black ribbon through each of the top holes in the plates and one through each of the bottom holes; they will hold the costume in place.

5 With black tape, make balls on the ends of the pipe cleaners and tape the pipe cleaners to the black baseball cap.

6 After the child has dressed in the oversized sweatshirt, put a pillow inside the sweatshirt on her back. Arrange the costume on the front of the child. Criss-cross the ribbon straps against her back to hold the pillow in place and to secure the costume on her shoulders and waist.

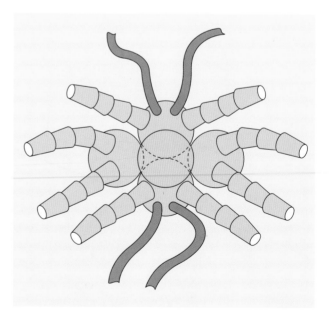

Steps 1 to 4. Make diamond of 4 black plates and a central red one. Attach legs as shown. Straps tie around child.

Welcome to my web.

Cell Phone

You rang?

MATERIALS

- twelve 12 oz (360 mL) white plastic cups
- two 6½" × 27" (16.5 × 68.5 cm) pieces of foam core board
- 6½" × 15" (16.5 × 38 cm) foam core board
- 15" × 27" (38 × 68.5 cm) foam core board
- 2" × 15" (5 × 38 cm) foam core board
- 12" × 15" (30.5 × 38 cm) foam core board
- 9" × 15" (23 × 38 cm) foam core board
- two 12½" × 7" (32 × 18 cm) pieces of foam core board
- 12½" × 15" (32 × 38 cm) foam core board
- 3" × 10" (7. 5 × 25.5 cm) cardboard tube
- 12" × 28" (30.5 × 71 cm) black wrapping paper
- three rolls of ½" (1.2 cm) wide black tape
- 8 oz (240 mL) bottle black acrylic paint
- 3 oz (90 mL) bottle white acrylic paint
- 4" × 4" (10 × 10 cm) disposable plastic container with lid
- white glue
- 2" (5 cm) wide clear packing tape
- computer printout or hand-lettered sign with the word "TALK" (letters about ¾" or 2 cm tall)
- computer printouts or hand-lettered keypad numbers and letters (numbers should be 1" or 2.5 cm tall and letters, ½" or 1 cm).

TOOLS: craft knife, medium-wide paintbrush or 3" (7.5 cm) cotton roller, ruler, pencil, scissors

CHILD WEARS: black shirt, red or contrasting color pants, black shoes

DIRECTIONS

1 Lay out the number pad with ruled pencil lines as shown in the diagram:

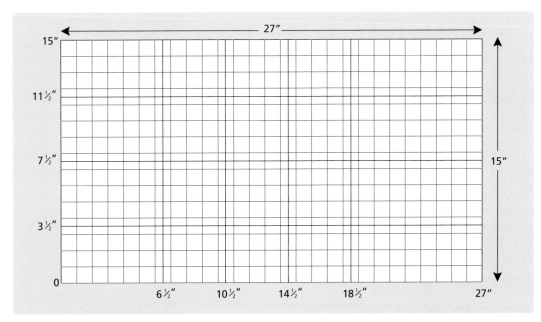

Step 1. Rule foam core board as shown. 1 box = 1" (2.5 cm). Places where black lines cross are locations of buttons.

1a Take the 15" × 27" (38 × 68.5 cm) foam core board and lay the board with the long edge facing you. Place marks on both the near and far long edges at 6½" (16.5 cm), 10½" (26.5 cm), 14½" (37 cm), and 18½" (47 cm) from the left edge.

1b Connect these marks by drawing lines from the 6½" (16.5 cm) near mark to the 6½" far mark. In the same way, connect the near and far marks at 10½", 14½", and 18½", leaving you with four 15" (38 cm) long parallel lines that are 4" (10 cm) apart from each other.

1c Next place marks at 3½" (9 cm), 7½" (19 cm), and 11½" (29 cm) on the left and right edges, measuring from the bottom edge up.

1d Connect the marks on the left edge to the marks on the right edge by ruled lines, leaving you with three 27" (68.5 cm) long parallel lines connecting the two sides, with 4" (10 cm) between them.

1e The left edge will be the top of the number pad and the right edge will be the bottom of the number pad.

2 You should have 7 lines that cross at 12 points. Use the bottom of one of your 12 oz

(360 mL) cups to trace a circle that is centered over every crossing point. Cut out the circles with a craft knife. These circles will be where you will put your buttons for the number pad.

3 Clear-tape one long edge of each 6½" × 27" (16.5 × 68.5 cm) piece of foam core to each long edge of the 15" × 27" (38 × 68.5 cm) number pad.

4 Tape a long edge of the 6½" × 15" (16.5 × 38 cm) piece of foam core to the bottom edge of the number pad and to the bottom edges of the sides of the number pad to complete the main frame of the phone.

5 To create the earpiece (where the face hole is), refer to diagrams for Steps 5 and 6:

5a Make a 7½" × 8½" (19 × 21.5 cm) oval cutout in the center of the 12½" × 15" (32 × 38 cm) piece of foam core board (see diagram).

5b Tape the long edge of the 2" × 15" (5 × 38 cm) piece of foam core board to the lower 15" (38 cm) edge of the piece of foam core board with the oval cutout. (All taping joins boards at right angles.) The 2" wide piece will act as the bottom edge of the earpiece.

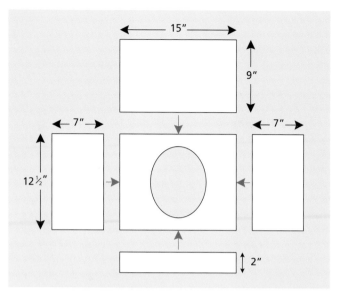

Step 5b, c, d. Assemble earpiece as shown, taping sides at right angles to central panel.

5c Tape one long edge of each 7" × 12½" (18 × 32 cm) piece to the 12½" sides of the piece with the cutout and to the 2" bottom (see diagram).

5d Then tape one 15" (38 cm) edge of the 9" × 15" (23 × 38 cm) piece of foam core to the top 15" edge of the piece with the oval cutout. Tape the 9" sides to the 7" sides of the 7" × 12½" pieces. See diagram.

6 Tape the earpiece to the number pad with the earpiece's 2" (5 cm) side towards the number pad (see diagram).

7 Paint the entire phone black. Let dry.

8 Use black tape on all of the corners and edges to make nice clean lines (don't forget to tape the edges of the oval).

9 From the back of the costume, push the plastic cups though the holes in the number pad to create the buttons for the phone and tape them in place on the back, using the 2" (5 cm) wide clear packing tape.

10 Paint the 4" × 4" (10 × 10 cm) lid and container with the white acrylic paint and let dry.

11 Glue the painted 4" (10 cm) container in the upper left portion of the number pad, above the #1 button. This container will be the "push to talk" button.

12 Glue the painted 4" lid to the bottom middle portion of the number pad (below the 0 button). This will be the mouthpiece of the phone.

13 Use the 3" × 10" (7.5 × 25.5 cm) tube to trace a circle on the top of the earpiece where an antenna would go. Cut out the circle.

14 Wrap the 3" × 10" tube with black wrapping paper. Push tube through the antenna hole and tape from the inside with the 2" (5 cm) wide clear packing tape.

15 Cut out and paste the word "TALK" on the "push to talk" button, and then cut out and paste the numbers and letters for the keypad on the appropriate buttons.

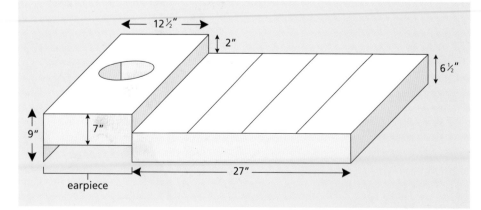

Step 6. Side view of cell phone, showing earpiece attached to body of phone.

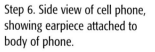

Corn on the Cob

You could be accused of being corny.

MATERIALS

- 24" × 48" (61 × 122 cm) piece of corrugated cardboard
- 20" × 20" (51 × 51 cm) piece of corrugated cardboard
- four 2" × 30" (5 × 76 cm) strips of cardboard
- roll of clear packing tape
- two hundred ¾ oz (22 mL) plastic soufflé cups (the kind used for salad dressing)
- 8 oz (237 mL) yellow acrylic paint
- four packages (of at least 12 sheets each) green tissue paper 24" × 36" (61 × 91.5 cm)
- three packages (of at least 12 sheets each) yellow tissue paper 24" × 36" (61 × 91.5 cm)
- bottle of white glue

TOOLS: scissors, craft knife, paintbrush, ruler, pencil

CHILD WEARS: jeans, boots, white T-shirt

This is a great costume for your harvest parade. Dress the other kids as scarecrows and old black crows to make it fun for all members of the family.

DIRECTIONS

1 Create a cylinder with the 24" × 48" (61 × 122 cm) piece of cardboard and secure it by taping the 24" edges together from top to the bottom.

2 Place the cardboard cylinder on top of the 20" × 20" (51 × 51 cm) piece of cardboard. Trace around the cylinder and cut the circle out to make a lid. Tape the lid to the top of cylinder.

3 Attach the four 2" × 30" (5 × 76 cm) strips of cardboard around the lid, folding in the middle to make a point; this will make the top of the corn.

4 To fit the costume to the child, cut a 1" (2.5 cm) peephole where you think his face will be when he will wear the costume. Then place the cylinder over the child's head to figure out where to cut out the final holes for the face and arms. Look in the peephole that you cut in the costume and use a pencil to draw an oval on the outside of the cylinder that is approximately the size of your child's face. Also try to see where you want the armholes to be and trace the circles that you will cut out. Remove the costume and cut out the holes.

5 Make a center panel on the cylinder about 8" (20 cm) wide and 24" (61 cm) tall by taping down the yellow tissue paper. Tape yellow tissue paper to the top of the costume, covering the entire point.

6 Cover the rest of the costume with green tissue paper, taking care to keep it all flat and maintain clean lines. Tape using the 2" (5 cm) clear packing tape.

7 You will now need to glue the soufflè cups (representing corn kernels) to the yellow tissue. Lay the cylinder flat on your work area. Glue on the soufflé cups in rows. The soufflé cups will need to dry overnight. Prop your cylinder so it won't move.

Steps 1 to 3. Making the cylinder. Fold strips in half and tape to the lid to make the point.

8 The next day, paint your soufflé cups with yellow acrylic paint. Cover all visible sides of the soufflé cups completely. Let this dry for an hour.

9 To make the corn silk, layer three sheets of yellow tissue paper and fold in half so that you have a folded stack that is 12" × 36" (30.5 × 91.5 cm). Cut these stacks into thirty-six 1" × 12" (2.5 × 30.5 cm) folded stacks of strips, being careful to keep the sheets together. Repeat the process until you've cut up four 3-sheet stacks of tissue paper. Tape the folded end of each bundle of strips to the point of the cylinder. Cover the whole top point of the costume with yellow strips, allowing the edges to fall outwards from the point. Use all of the bundles.

10 Using three sheets of tissue paper at a time, cut out thirty 6" × 18" (15 × 45.5 cm) strips of green tissue. Round one end on all of the green strips that have been cut out. This goes quicker if you keep the sheets stacked while cutting.

11 Start at the top of costume. Scrunch the green tissue in one hand to give it body and tape the 6" × 18" (15 × 45.5 cm) strips to cover the upper part of the ear of corn, with the rounded edges up and fluttering. Then, taping on row by row of green tissue paper, work down the costume, keeping ½" (1.2 cm) between rows, until you reach the bottom of the costume.

12 Tape any leftover green tissue strips to the costume near the bottom edge, allowing them to hang off the costume.

Cupcake

Just as cute as a cupcake!

MATERIALS

- circular plastic laundry basket, 24" (61 cm) in diameter*
- 18" (46 cm) white shoelace
- 5" × 24" (12.4 × 61 cm) piece of white cotton fabric
- 24" (61 cm) red ricrac
- 24" × 24" (61 × 61 cm) piece of corrugated cardboard
- 2" (5 cm) diameter cardboard tube, 24" (61 cm) long
- one sheet of 12" × 18" (30.5 × 45.5 cm) construction paper in: yellow, blue, and orange
- 7" × 28" (18 × 71 cm) yellow wrapping paper
- 2" (5 cm) wide clear packing tape
- roll of 18" (30.5 cm) wide aluminum foil, enough to surround basket twice
- 28" × 28" (71 × 71 cm) piece of polyurethane foam batting
- 28" × 28" (71 × 71 cm) pink T-shirt fabric
- plastic headband

*Laundry basket should be wide enough to fit around child's torso.

TOOLS: saw, scissors, marker, craft knife, pencil, hot glue gun, ruler, ruling compass

CHILD WEARS: white tights and shoes

DIRECTIONS

1 Cut out bottom of laundry basket with saw.

2 Turn basket upside down and lay the top edge of laundry basket flush on a 24" × 24" (61 × 61 cm) piece of cardboard, or whatever size will be larger than the top of the opening. Trace around the basket edge with pencil. Cut the traced circle out.

3 Cut out a 9" (23 cm) diameter circle right in the center of the circle you just cut from the piece of cardboard.

4 Using 2" (5 cm) wide clear packing tape, carefully tape the cardboard circle to the top of the laundry basket.

5 Lay foam batting on the work table. Turn the basket upside down on it. With a marker, trace around the cardboard circle onto the batting. Draw another circle 3" (7.5 cm) wider than the circle outline, and cut the wider circle out of the batting.

6 Use hot glue to attach the T-shirt material to the top of the foam batting, trimming the fabric's edges into the circle shape.

7 Turn the basket right-side up and hot-glue the foam batting to the top of the cardboard on the basket, turning the edges of the batting and fabric underneath while gluing to give a fluffy appearance. Cut out an 8" (20 cm) diameter hole in the center of the fluffy batting for the child's head. Turn any excess batting to the inside of the cardboard circle and hot-glue it to the cardboard circle so there are no loose edges.

8 Stack the 12" × 18" (30.5 × 45.5 cm) yellow, blue, and orange sheets of construction paper. Draw 1" (2.5 cm) diameter circles all over the top sheet. Keeping the sheets carefully stacked, cut out the 1" (2.5 cm) circles so that you have some colorful decorations to put on top of the cupcake.

9 Take the 18" (45.5 cm) wide aluminum foil and fold in each short side 1" (2.5 cm) to round off the edges. Then use the 2" (5 cm) packing tape to tape the aluminum foil to the sides of the laundry basket. To create a ridged look like a cupcake wrapper, as shown in the photo, tape every 3" (7.5 cm) and fold the aluminum foil like an accordion as you go around the cupcake (see photo).

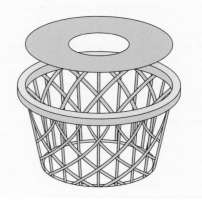

Steps 1 to 3. Basket has bottom carefully cut away. Circle for top has 9" (23 cm) diameter circle cut away in center.

10 Hot-glue the orange, yellow, and blue construction paper circles to look like confetti all over the top of the foam batting.

11 Take the 2" × 24" (5 × 30.5 cm) cardboard tube and wrap with yellow wrapping paper to make a candle for the cupcake.

12 Drip hot glue on the top and sides of the yellow candle to imitate melting wax. Let dry.

13 Tape the bottom of the candle to the headband with 2" (5 cm) wide clear packing tape.

14 To make the ruffled collar, take the 5" × 24" (12.5 × 61 cm) white cotton fabric and fold in 1" (2.5 cm) on the long side. Hot-glue the edge down along the 24" (61 cm) side to make a 1" wide casing for the shoelace. On the other long side of fabric, hot-glue the strip of ricrac. Let dry.

15 Slip the shoelace through the casing. Tie the collar around child's neck after she slips the cupcake costume on.

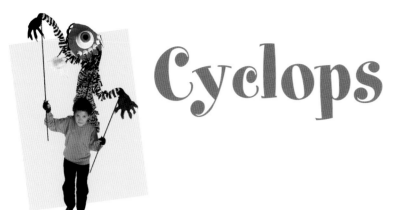

Cyclops

MATERIALS

- two sets of knit black gloves
- 12" (30.5 cm) diameter plastic trick-or-treat pumpkin
- two ³⁄₈" × 48" (1 × 122 cm) wooden dowels
- ½" × 32" (1.2 × 81 cm) wooden dowel
- ½" (1.2 cm) black tape
- 12 oz (360 mL) black plastic cup or black paper
- ½" (1.2 cm) wide red tape
- letter-size piece of green paper
- acrylic paint: white, green, and black
- six 1 oz (30 mL) parfait cups
- 8 oz (237 mL) plastic bowl
- seven 18" (45.5 cm) black pipe cleaners
- 3 oz (90 mL) bag white marabou feathers
- 28" × 36" (71 × 91.5 cm) fuzzy orange fabric
- two 100" (254 cm) lengths of 18 gauge wire
- two 30" (76 cm) lengths of wire to attach head
- ³⁄₄" (2 cm) × 12" (30.5 cm) PVC pipe
- ³⁄₄" (2 cm) PVC T connector
- ³⁄₄" (2 cm) PVC 4-way connector
- two 2" × 56" (5 × 142 cm) black fabric strips
- two 8" × 36" (20 × 91.5 cm) pieces of black/white striped fabric (stripes go across 8" dimension) for sleeves
- black thread
- 24" × 36" (61 × 91.5 cm) piece of colorful striped fabric for body
- PVC pipe glue (optional)
- tacky glue
- three sheets of newspaper

TOOLS: wire cutters, drill with ¹⁄₈" (3 mm) drill bit, needle, hot glue gun, paintbrush, ruler

CHILD WEARS: orange long-sleeved sweatshirt, black pants and shoes

DIRECTIONS

1 Drill six ¹⁄₈" (3 mm) holes in the plastic pumpkin, just below the rim, spaced evenly around the opening, near the edge.

2 Drill four ¹⁄₈" (3 mm) holes, 1½", 3½", 12", and 13½" (4 cm, 9 cm, 30 cm, and 34 cm) down from one end of the ½" (1.2 cm) wide dowel. The dowel will be the body on which the head and arms are mounted.

3a To attach the head, take a 30" (76 cm) piece of wire and feed it halfway through the top hole in the dowel; then twist the wire parts together close to the dowel, leaving two equal lengths of wire facing out from the sides of the dowel. Feed one wire end through each of two holes on one side of the pumpkin (see diagram),

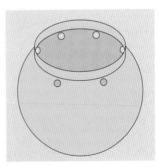

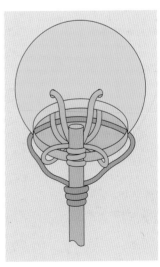

Step 1. Make 6 holes, evenly spaced, around the rim of the pumpkin.

Step 3a and b. Attach pumpkin to dowel with 2 pieces of wire.

Beware of one-eyed monsters!

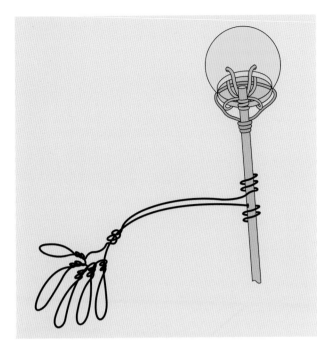

Step 4. Shaping an arm and a hand.

securing it around the dowel. Feed the other wire end through two holes on the other side of the pumpkin in the same way.

3b Take another 30" (76 cm) long wire and feed through the two remaining holes in the pumpkin. Feed one of the wire ends through the second hole in the dowel and twist the wire around dowel to secure. Bring the remaining wire end back to the dowel and twist around it for extra strength. Head should bobble.

4 Take a 100" (254 cm) piece of wire and thread one end a few inches (5 or 7 cm) through the third hole in the dowel. Twist the short end of the wire around the dowel to anchor it. This wire will become one arm and hand of the costume.

5 About 22" (56 cm) down the 100" (254 cm) wire, start to shape a hand. After shaping each finger, twist wire together at base of finger. When finished with hand, twist wire around where wrist would be. Bring excess wire back to

dowel. Twist remaining wire around dowel. Shape the second hand and arm using the second piece of 100" wire, the same way as the first one, but starting the wire in the fourth hole down on the dowel.

6 Hot-glue seven black pipe cleaners to the top of the orange head. Hot-glue white feathers to the ends of the black pipe cleaners.

7 Cover plastic pumpkin with hot glue. Drape the 28" × 36" (71 × 91.5 cm) fuzzy orange fabric over pumpkin so it covers the whole thing, and hot-glue in place, shaping the fabric around the pipe cleaners and letting some fabric hang down a few inches (5 or 7 cm) below the pumpkin edge to form a neck and cover the wires.

8 Paint the plastic bowl and six parfait cups white with acrylic paint on the undersides. Let dry.

9 From a black plastic cup or black paper, cut out six ¼" × 4" (0.5 × 10 cm) pointed shapes (see photo). Tape one sharp black point to the center of each white 1 oz (30 mL) parfait cup with red tape.

10 Tacky-glue parfait cups to the front of the orange fuzzy head in the shape of a smile.

11 To make the eye, on the bottom of the white plastic bowl, paint a green circle; then paint a black circle dead center of the green circle. Tacky-glue the bowl above the smile on the fuzzy orange head to create the Cyclops' eye.

12 Fold an 8" × 36" (20 × 91.5 cm) black-and-white striped piece of fabric in half so that it is 4" × 36" (10 × 91.5 cm). Sew the 36" (91.5 cm) edges closed to create a sleeve for one of the arms of the costume. Repeat on the other 8" × 36" (20 × 91.5 cm) piece of fabric.

13 Turn the black-and-white sleeves right-side out so that stitching is on the inside. Slip one over each wire arm. Sew one sleeve end to the base of the orange head on the orange fabric.

14 Place a black glove on each wire hand and stuff with small pieces of newspaper to fill out. Tape the glove to the striped arm with black tape. Repeat for the second hand.

15 Wrap the 48" (122 cm) dowels with black tape.

16 Wrap the wrist of the stuffed glove with black tape, and tape the dowel to the glove at the wrist, so that the child can manipulate the arm by moving the other end of the dowel. Repeat on the second wire hand.

17 To make the body, fold the 24" × 36" (61 × 91.5 cm) colorful striped fabric in half with right sides facing, making it 12" × 36" (30.5 × 91.5 cm). Sew the 36" (91.5 cm) sides closed and turn right-side out. Slip this body over the dowel that has the Cyclops head, and hot-glue the end of the striped fabric to the fuzzy orange head.

18 Cut up the green paper to make 20 pointy claws. Hot-glue claws on top of the fingers on the gloves of the Cyclops and on an extra set of gloves for the child.

19 Connect the 12" (30.5 cm) PVC pipe to a T connector. Connect the other side of the 12" (30.5 cm) PVC pipe to a PVC 4-way connector. For a more permanent connection, you can use PVC pipe glue, if you wish.

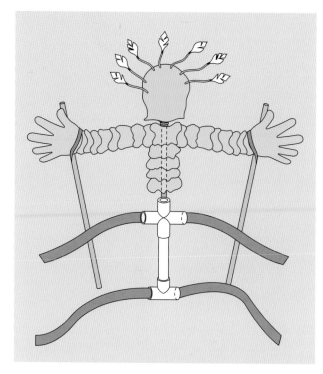

Steps 20 and 21. Back view showing assembled costume. Fabric strips are inserted through PVC connectors. Dowel is slipped through top of 4-way connector.

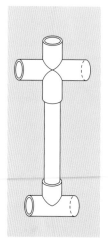

Step 19. PVC tubing in PVC connectors.

20 Place the 12" (30.5 cm) length of PVC pipe so it is centered on the child's back. Thread the 2" × 56" (5 × 142 cm) length of black fabric through the PVC frame's 4-way connector and criss-cross the fabric over the chest. Thread a second length of 2" × 56" (5 × 142 cm) black fabric through the T connector, and tie around the child to secure the costume. Have child put on sweatshirt.

21 Slip the bottom of the dowel that holds the Cyclops' head and arms through the top of the PVC 4-way connector on the child's back.

22 The child wears black gloves on his hands and moves the monster's hands by moving the black dowels.

Fangs and Claws

MATERIALS

- 24" × 48" (61 × 122 cm) piece of corrugated cardboard
- four 24" × 24" (61 × 61 cm) pieces of corrugated cardboard
- 2" × 10" (5 × 25.5 cm) piece of corrugated cardboard
- nineteen Styrofoam coffee cups
- four Plastifoam™ 4" × 9" (10 × 23 cm) white plastic cones
- 5 yards (4.5 m) red wrapping paper
- two 6" (15 cm) Styrofoam balls
- 2" (5 cm) Styrofoam egg
- black plastic plate or black cardboard
- two blue plastic Easter eggs
- 6" × 18" (30.5 × 45.5 cm) white construction paper for claws
- 1½" (3.8 cm) wide red tape
- 2" (5 cm) wide clear packing tape
- five toothpicks
- two orange 54" × 108" (137 × 274 cm) plastic tablecloths
- orange acrylic paint
- two 15" (38 cm) ribbons to tie paws to child's arms

TOOLS: craft knife, scissors, paintbrush, ruling compass or large dish, hot glue gun

CHILD WEARS: all red sweatsuit

DIRECTIONS

1 Fold one 24" × 48" (61 × 122 cm) piece of cardboard in half so its folded size is 24" × 24" (61 × 61 cm). It is now a "V" shape. Set it aside.

2 Using a craft knife, score two of the 24" × 24" (61 × 61 cm) squares of cardboard on one side, 2" (5 cm) in from one edge, across the width of the side. Be careful not to cut too deeply; you should just break the upper surface of the cardboard with the craft knife. Fold each piece of cardboard along the score mark at a 90° angle to make a 2" (5 cm) flap.

3 To create the lips of the monster, tape the edges of one 2" × 24" (5 × 61 cm) cardboard flap to the outside edges of the folded 24" × 48" (61 × 122 cm) piece (see diagram). Tape the bottom part of the 24" × 24" (61 × 61 cm) piece of cardboard near the fold of the 24" × 48" (61 × 122 cm) piece of cardboard. Tape the second piece of 24" × 24" (61 × 61 cm) cardboard on the other side of the 24" × 48" (61 × 122 cm) cardboard in the same way. Now you have a cardboard "V" with folded edges.

4 Trace and cut out a large round circle in the center of the lower half of the cardboard "V" through both layers of cardboard. The circle should be big enough for a child's head to go through. Use the compass (or plate) and a craft knife.

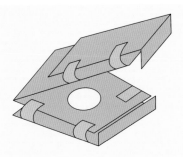

Steps 3 and 4. Cardboards with 2" (5 cm) edges are taped to the V-shaped cardboard. Circles are cut through the bottom two cardboard layers.

Does someone need his morning coffee?

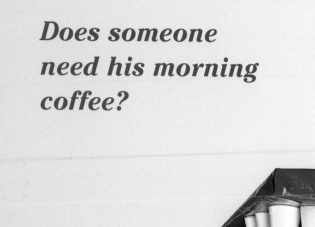

5 Wrap the whole "V" frame with red wrapping paper. Cut away the paper covering the hole for child's head and tape down loose paper.

6 On the inside of the "V" frame, near the front, glue white cones for fangs, two on top in front, and two on bottom (see photo). Glue in Styrofoam cups to look like teeth also. Let dry.

7 Take a 2" × 10" (5 × 25.5 cm) piece of cardboard and stick a toothpick straight through the cardboard into a 6" (15 cm) Styrofoam ball to make an eye. Place the other 6" ball next to the first eye (leave a little room in between for a nose) and join it to the cardboard in the same way. Glue the toothpicks in place so they stay well.

8 Paint a Styrofoam egg orange and attach it with a toothpick and glue in between the 6" (15 cm) Styrofoam balls, for a nose.

9 Tape the 2" × 10" (5 × 25.5 cm) cardboard that has the eyes and nose to the top edge of the "V" frame, near the front, using red tape.

10 With hot glue, stick a blue Easter egg onto each 6" (15 cm) Styrofoam eyeball.

11 Cut out two 2" × 8" (5 × 20 cm) black strips from black plastic plates or cardboard. Hot-glue each to the top of a 6" (15 cm) Styrofoam eye ball to be an eyebrow.

12 For claws, mark out twelve 4¼" × 4¼" × 6" (10.8 × 10.8 × 15.2 cm) triangles on the 6" × 18" (15 × 45.5 cm) white construction paper and cut them out.

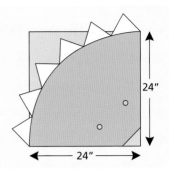

Step 13. Grid for drawing and cutting out paw boards. 1 box = 4" (10 cm). Black dot = hole for ribbon. Swing an arc from corner to corner that fits all the claws. Cut away gray parts.

13 For paws, lay 6 claw triangles on a 24" × 24" (61 × 61 cm) piece of cardboard (see diagram). Draw an arc from one corner of the cardboard to its diagonally opposite corner to make a quarter circle. This should make a large paw, large enough to fit all 6 claws, but don't attach them yet. Cut out the paw shape, trimming off the corner (see diagram). Make another paw on the other 24" × 24" (61 × 61 cm) cardboard.

14 Cover each paw board front and back with part of the orange tablecloth, gluing and taping it in place.

15 Glue and tape 6 white triangles as claws on each paw board.

16 Tape a 1" (2.5 cm) tall red tip around the point of each claw with red tape.

17 Poke 2 holes about 4" (10 cm) apart, about 8 inches (20 cm) in from the end of the paw (see diagram for Step 13). String a ribbon through the paw holes and tie each paw to the child's arm (see photo).

Fireworks

Start the celebration!

MATERIALS

- 17" × 17" (43 × 43 cm) piece of corrugated cardboard
- two 14" × 36" (35.5 × 91.5 cm) pieces of corrugated cardboard
- lightweight wire tomato tower (trellis), round or square
- seven rolls of decorative star wire garland
- four 20" (51 cm) shooting star cone decorations
- 28" × 6' (71 × 183 cm) aluminum foil
- four 1" × 2" × 16½" (2.5 × 5 × 42 cm) wooden stakes
- four 2" (5 cm) diameter × 6" (15 cm) wooden dowels
- four large screw eyes (trellis leg must fit through eye)
- 28" × 6' (71 × 183 cm) red wrapping paper
- eight 1" (2.5 cm) drywall screws
- four 2" (5 cm) drywall screws
- 12" × 18" (30.5 × 45.5 cm) sheets of construction paper: 1 of yellow, 1 of red; 1 of blue, 2 of gold, 2 of silver, 1 of white
- white glue
- Chinese style rice-farmer's straw hat, or paper hat
- 2" (5 cm) wide clear packing tape
- two 36" (91.5 cm) lengths of strong ribbon for shoulder straps; color to match shirt

TOOLS: pliers, diagonal-cutting pliers or wire cutters, staple gun, screwdriver, drill and drill bits, scissors

CHILD WEARS: a silver top or red shirt covered in silver stars, blue jeans, and white shoes

DIRECTIONS

1 Pinch off the lowest horizontal round or bar on the tomato trellis all around, leaving the top three so there is room for the child to stand.

2 Turn the tomato trellis upside down and trace the top of the trellis (may be a circle or another shape) onto a 17" × 17" (43 × 43 cm) piece of cardboard, or whatever size you need for the top. Cut out the traced shape and wrap with aluminum foil. This will be the top of the fireworks.

3 Poke 3 holes in the top of the fireworks. Insert the bottoms of the 20" (51 cm) shooting star decorations into the fireworks top so they hang upside down, and clear-tape them to the fireworks top. Set aside the top of the fireworks for now.

4 Wrap the entire tomato trellis with star garlands.

5 Stack the red, yellow, silver, gold, white, and blue construction paper. On the top sheet draw as many star shapes as will fit, and cut out the stars through all layers.

Step 1. Tomato trellis with one round cut away, or as many as are needed for child to have room to stand.

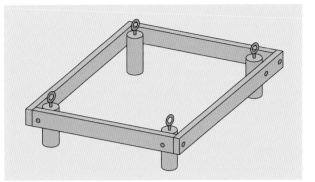

Step 9. Assembled frame has dowels with screw eyes in their tops.

6 Wrap the straw hat with aluminum foil and secure the foil with clear tape.

7 Wrap each of the 14" × 36" (35.5 × 91.5 cm) cardboard pieces with red wrapping paper and tape paper in place. Glue large white and blue paper stars in a row to the middle of the covered cardboard. These pieces of cardboard will be stapled to the wooden frame for sides to the box part of the costume.

8 Place silver stars and gold stars back to back and glue to wire garlands on the tomato trellis. The more stars glued, the merrier.

9 With the four wooden stakes, create a wooden frame on which to mount the tomato trellis, using two of the 1" (2.5 cm) drywall screws to join the stakes together at each corner. Glue a dowel section inside each corner, adding a 2" (5 cm) screw through the frame near each corner for added strength.

10 Drill a hole in the top of each dowel section and insert a screw eye in each. These screw eyes will be used to anchor the trellis in the wooden frame.

11 Flip the tomato trellis and wooden frame onto their sides. Using the pliers, wrap the wire end of each leg of the tomato trellis through one of the screw eyes on the dowels and around itself to secure it. Cover any sharp ends with tape. Be sure all the trellis legs end up being the same length.

12 For straps, tie two 36" (91.5 cm) lengths of strong ribbon to the front of the wooden frame, about 10" (25 cm) apart. Then cross them diagonally and tie them onto the back of the frame, adjusting them to your child's height so they hold the costume on the shoulders.

13 Using the staple gun, staple the 14" × 36" (35.5 × 91.5 cm) cardboard pieces you decorated in Step 7 to the wooden frame as box sides, bending them as necessary to go around corners. Cover all 4 sides of the frame. The cardboard should extend up a few inches (3 to 6 cm) above the frame, so the dowels and frame don't show.

14 With clear packing tape, attach the aluminum-foil-covered top of the trellis from Step 3.

15 Make the costume as festive as you want by scattering stars around the costume.

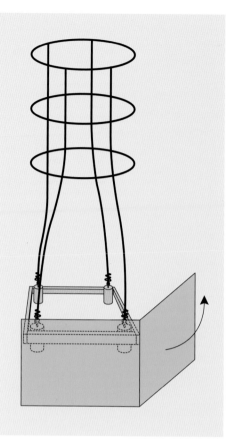

Step 13. Staple cardboard side to frame so it hides dowels; bend cardboard at corner.

Basket of Flowers

MATERIALS

- 24" (61 cm) wide wicker laundry basket*
- fifty-six 8 oz (240 mL) Styrofoam coffee cups
- five 1-gallon (3.8 L) plastic water jugs
- twenty-eight colored plastic Easter eggs
- acrylic paint, 2.5 oz (75 mL) size: yellow, orange, pink, and purple
- fifty-six green pipe cleaners
- twenty 12" × 18" (30.5 × 45.5 cm) sheets of green tissue paper
- 2" (5 cm) wide clear packing tape
- plastic headband
- two 2" × 24" (5 × 61 cm) strips of strong green cotton fabric or green ribbon
- tacky glue
- 1" (2.5 cm) wide green tape

*Laundry basket must be wide enough for child to wear around torso.

TOOLS: scissors, saw, ruler, paintbrush

CHILD WEARS: green or black sweatshirt, tan pants, and white shoes

DIRECTIONS

1 Cut away the bottom from a 24" (61 cm) laundry basket with a saw. Make sure to cut away only the inside of the bottom; cut as close to the edge binding as possible without cutting the binding.

2 To make small flowers, cut ½" (1.2 cm) wide strips into the Styrofoam cups, starting around the rim and stopping about ½" (1.2 cm) up from the bottom of cup. Do this to all 56 cups.

3 Paint the insides of the small flower cups with hot pink, purple, orange, and yellow acrylic paint. Use one color per cup. Do not paint the white edges of cup. Let dry.

4 Take one-half of a colored Easter egg and run tacky glue around the open edge of the egg. Glue each half in the center of a painted Styrofoam cup. Let dry. Repeat this for all 56 cups. Make sure that the color of the egg is not the same as the color of the inside of the cup. A good combination is a light color on top of a dark color or a dark color on top of a light one.

5 Cut the green tissue paper into fifty-six 4" × 12" (10 × 30.5 cm) strips for leaves. Fold each tissue paper strip in half and tape it with green tape along with a green pipe cleaner end to the back of a cup. The green pipe cleaners will be the flower stems. Do this to all 56 cups. Set aside.

6 Take all five 1-gallon (3.8 L) water jugs and cut the bottom off each. Shape the sides with scissors to look like tulip petals. Paint the

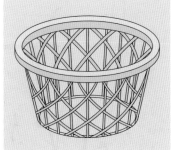

Step 1. Bottom of basket is cut away.

Step 6. Trim the sides of the water jug to make a tulip shape. Shaded parts and bottom are cut away.

Win someone's heart by bringing her flowers.

petals with color. Let dry. Tape the mouth of the water jug with green tape to look like the stem of a tulip. Tie pipe cleaners and green tissue paper around the mouth of each water-jug tulip.

7 Decide which side will be the front of costume. Insert the green pipe cleaner stem of each small flower in the basket rim and twist the pipe cleaner around itself to hold it in place. Attach your flowers side by side in the same way until they go completely around the front of basket.

8 Make another row of flowers above the first row. Lightly tape the rows together with clear packing tape to secure. Be sure to save some flowers for the headband.

9 For shoulder straps, take 2" × 24" (5 × 61 cm) strips of green fabric or ribbon and tie one end of each onto the front of the basket through the rim. They should be about 10" (25 cm) apart. Slip the loose end of one strip of the green fabric through the handles of half the water-jug tulips. Do the same thing for the second fabric strip with the rest of the water-jug tulips. Criss-cross the straps and tie the loose ends of the green fabric strips onto the rim at the back of the basket, about 10" apart from each other. Slip the basket over the child's head and adjust the strap length as needed.

10 Fold twelve 4" × 12" (10 × 30.5 cm) strips of green tissue paper in half. Wrap tissue paper around the straps; this is easiest to do when child is already in costume.

11 Wrap the headband with green tape. Twist the pipe cleaner stems of a few flowers made of Styrofoam cups around the headband, and tape flowers in place with clear packing tape (see photo).

Frankenstein's Monster

MATERIALS

- 8" × 14" × 16" (20 × 35.5 × 40.6 cm) cardboard box
- 12" × 12" × 30" (30.5 × 30.5 × 76 cm) cardboard box
- 6" × 10" × 32" (15 × 25.5 × 81 cm) cardboard box
- 18" × 24" (45.5 × 61 cm) piece of corrugated cardboard
- 54" × 108" (137 × 274 cm) green plastic tablecloth
- 54" × 108" (137 × 274 cm) purple plastic tablecloth
- two 8 oz (240 mL) purple plastic bowls
- eight 10" (25.5 cm) black plastic plates
- 10" (25.5 cm) yellow plastic plate
- 10" (25.5 cm) white plastic plate
- four 8" (20 cm) diameter orange plastic plates
- two 12 oz (360 mL) black plastic cups
- five 12 oz (360 mL) red plastic cups
- dome lid for 12 oz (360 mL) plastic cup
- two 3 oz (90 mL) plastic cups
- 24" × 24" (61 × 61 cm) piece of aluminum foil
- 2" (5 cm) wide clear packing tape
- ½" (1.2 cm) wide yellow tape
- tacky glue
- white glue
- red acrylic paint

TOOLS: scissors, pencil, ½" (1.2 cm) paint-brush, ruler, 3" (7.5 cm) paint roller, craft knife

CHILD WEARS: black pants, black shirt and shoes

DIRECTIONS

1 Tape all the boxes so that their flaps are closed. Lay the 12" × 12" × 30" (30.5 × 30.5 × 76 cm) box on the work surface on its largest side, so its length is vertical to you; it will become the face box. Place the 8" × 14" × 16" (20 × 35.5 × 40.6 cm) box horizontally on the work surface with one 16" (40.6 cm) side on the table, centered above the top end of the 12" × 12" × 30" box (see diagram). The smaller box will be the forehead of the costume. The forehead will stick out about 2" (5 cm) over the face and will extend beyond the sides of the face box. Tape the boxes together, using the 2" (5 cm) wide clear packing tape.

2 On the right side of the face box and 2" (5 cm) back from the front surface, mark a 6" deep and 10" wide (15 × 25.5 cm) rectangle, and cut it into the face box. Its lower edge should be flush with the bottom of the face box (see diagram). Its back edge should be flush with the back of the face box. Cut another rectangle the same way on the left side of the face box. The spaces you have cut will hold the shoulder box.

3 For the shoulders, push the 6" × 10" × 32" (15 × 25.5 × 81 cm) box into the spaces cut for the shoulders so that the long side of the box is running across

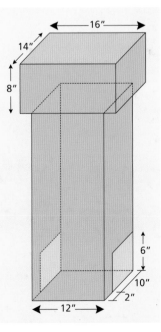

Step 2. Assembly of forehead box and face box. Gray part is cut away in face box to hold shoulder box.

inside and is centered in the face box. The 6"
(15 cm) side of the shoulder box should be
flush with the back of the face box. When
placed properly, the shoulder box should be
about 2" (5 cm) set back from the front of the
face box, and the shoulders should stick out 10"
(25.5 cm) to either side. Don't glue in place yet.

4 To lay out the 8" × 11" (20 × 27.5 cm) hole for
the mouth in the front of the face:

4a Make rules across the front of the face box,
7" (17.6 cm) and 18" (45.7 cm) up from the
bottom edge of the face box.

4b Measure in 2" (5 cm) from the edges of the
box on both lines and make marks for the
corners of the rectangle that you will cut out for
the mouth.

4c Rule vertical lines between the top (7") and
bottom (18") lines to finish the mouth
rectangle. Cut out the mouth from the cardboard.

4d Stand the costume upside down so its
lower end is up. In the bottom of the face box
and the shoulder box, cut a space that is large
enough for the child to fit in when he is wearing
the costume. Try the costume on the child;
be sure the child can see out and wear it
comfortably.

5 Remove the shoulder box from the costume.
Use the 3" (7.5 cm) paint roller to cover the
boxes for the face and forehead with white glue.
Then cover both boxes with large rectangles
cut from the green tablecloth. Tape the edges of
the tablecloth down with 2" (5 cm) wide clear
packing tape to create clean lines for the
costume. (Cover over the mouth hole when
wrapping.)

6 Clear the mouth hole by cutting through the
green tablecloth and trimming it to near the
edges of the hole. Then fold the excess tablecloth inside the box to create a clean edge, and
tape excess inside, using 2" (5 cm) wide clear
packing tape. Cut away the green tablecloth
that covers the side holes in the face box also.
Cover the shoulder box with part of the purple

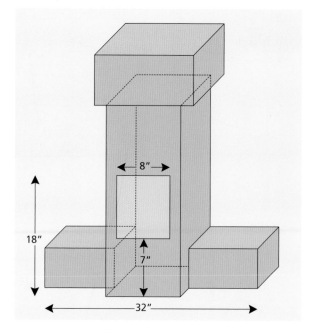

Steps 4 and 5. Shoulder box is inserted in face box. Window
for face is cut out (gray area).

tablecloth in the same way as for the other
boxes, and reinsert the shoulder box in position. Reserve enough purple plastic for the
chestplate.

7 Cut a 10" (25.5 cm) yellow plastic plate in
half. Then cut deep zigzags in each half to
create the monster's teeth.

8 Tape the half-plates with teeth inside the
mouth, using the yellow tape. Be careful to
make the teeth look menacing from the outside.

9 Paint the dome lid for the 12 oz (35.5 mL)
plastic cup using the red acrylic paint. Let it dry.

10 To create the nose, tape together three
12 oz (360 mL) red cups, stacking and taping
one inside of the other. Snap the dome lid on
the last cup to finish the nose.

11 Glue the nose to the center of the face
above the mouth with tacky glue (see photo).

12 Tacky-glue the purple bowls to each side of
the nose for eyes.

13 Cut out circles from white plastic plates to
make the whites of the monster's eyes. Tacky-
glue these to the eyes (purple bowls).

You are really in over your head this time!

14 Cut off bottoms of two 12 oz (360 mL) black plastic cups to make ½" (1.2 cm) tall black plastic disks for the centers of the eyes. Tacky-glue these to the white circles on the eyes.

15 Cover two 3 oz (90 mL) plastic cups and two 12 oz (360 mL) plastic cups with aluminum foil.

16 Tacky-glue the two 3 oz (90 mL) foil-covered cups to the forehead to look like bolts.

17 Use the bottoms of the 12 oz (360 mL) aluminum-foil-covered cups to trace circles 3" (7.5 cm) above the shoulders on the sides of the face box. Use scissors to cut out the circles. Then push the 12 oz (360 mL) foil-covered cups through the holes to make bolts for the sides of the face. Use 2" (5 cm) wide clear packing tape on the inside of the costume to secure the cups.

18 Cut a ¾" × 8" (2 × 20 cm) slit on each side of the head that is parallel to the face, starting 5" (12.5 cm) above the neck bolts. These slits will be used to hold the monster's ears.

19 Hold two 8" (20 cm) orange plastic plates face to face; then push these partway into one of the ear slits until the plates are properly seated. Tape them on the inside using 2" (5 cm) wide clear packing tape. Repeat the process for the second ear.

20 For the hair, cut six 10" (25 cm) black plastic plates in half. Cut ¾" (2 cm) wide strips down each half, starting from the straight edge, about 2½" (6.4 cm) deep. Don't cut the plate rims. Repeat this for all 12 halves.

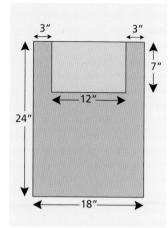

Step 23. Chestplate of costume. Gray area is cut away.

21 Tacky-glue the hair circle halves around the top of the forehead as shown in photo, being sure they adhere well to the box.

22 Cut the other two black plastic plates in half and cut out the half-circle bottoms; reserve the rims for eyebrows. Use the four half-circles to fill in extra spaces between the cut black plates, as needed. This should leave you with four half-rims from the plate edges. Without cutting all the way through to the outer edges, cut narrow strips into the ring, ¼" or ⅛" (5 mm or 3 mm) wide. Use for eyebrows. Trim to the right size and tacky-glue above the eyes.

23 Cut a rectangle 12" (30.5 cm) wide and 7" (18 cm) deep from one 18" side of the 18" × 24" (45.4 × 61 cm) cardboard, centering the rectangle on the width (it is 3" or 7.5 cm in from each edge). Cover the piece of cardboard with the remaining purple tablecloth. Trim and tape the edges of the tablecloth in place, using 2" (5 cm) wide clear packing tape. Try to keep clean lines on the edges. This will be the monster's chestplate.

24 You can tacky-glue the chestplate to the shoulders of the costume under the chin, to help stabilize the costume when it is worn. You can also attach a strap to the chestplate to go around the child's shoulders if you find that you need it.

Heart Box of Candy

MATERIALS

- two 36" × 36" (91.5 × 91.5 cm) pieces of corrugated cardboard
- 36" × 36" (91.5 × 91.5 cm) white paper
- two 12" × 48" (30.5 × 122 cm) pieces of corrugated cardboard
- 7' × 36" (213 × 91.5 cm) red wrapping paper
- three 24" × 24" (61 × 61 cm) sheets of black paper
- acrylic paint: 2.5 oz (75 mL) each of brown, hot pink, red, orange, and green
- 3 oz (85 g) acrylic gel medium
- 2" (5 cm) wide roll clear packing tape
- seven blocks of polyurethane foam, 2" × 5" × 8" (5 × 12.5 × 20.3 cm)
- four circles of polyurethane foam, 7" (18 cm) diameter × 2" (5 cm) thick
- glue

TOOLS: craft knife, scissors, small paintbrush, pencil, ruler

CHILD WEARS: white pants or tights, black shoes

DIRECTIONS

Making the Heart Box

1 On a 36" × 36" (91.5 × 91.5 cm) piece of cardboard, draw a large heart shape that uses as much of the area as possible, all the way out to the edges.

2 Cut out the heart shape to be the front panel of the heart and lay it on the second 36" × 36" (91.5 × 91.5 cm) piece of cardboard. Trace around the heart shape and cut out the heart to be the back of the box. On the 36" × 36" (91.5 × 91.5) white paper, trace and cut out a third heart. Set the paper heart aside.

3 On the front panel cardboard only, cut an 8" × 8" (20 × 20 cm) square out of the upper left area (see pattern). This will be where the child's face looks out of the costume.

4 Take a 12" × 48" (30.5 × 122 cm) piece of cardboard and start taping one long edge to the edge of the rear heart panel; continue taping it around the right half of the rear panel to make the side of the box. Tape it on the inside and

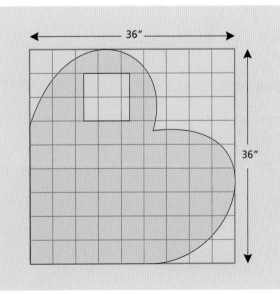

Step 1. Pattern for heart box front and back. 1 box = 4" (10 cm). Cut window in front only. Gray parts are cut away.

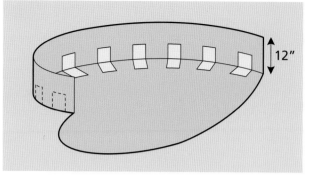

Step 4. Taping the edge to the back of heart.

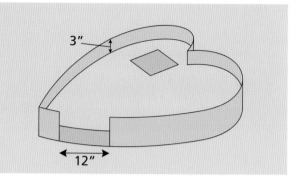

Steps 5 and 6. Front of heart box is recessed 3" (7.5 cm). Opening in side for child to stand is 12" (30.5 cm).

outside of the heart. Tape the other 12" × 48" (30.5 × 122 cm) piece of cardboard to the left half of the rear panel. Trim excess of 12" × 48" cardboard, if any.

5 Tape the front heart panel to the sides of the box, but be sure the front heart panel is recessed 3" (7.5 cm) from the side edges. The distance between the front and back will be 9" (23 cm).

6 On the bottom right of the heart, cut a 12" × 12" (30.5 × 30.5 cm) hole in the side wall of the box for the child's legs. This hole should be directly below the face hole in the top left corner. Try costume on child to see if she can fit into it, and check that the face can look out of the hole. Make any adjustments necessary.

7 After you are happy with the fit and have the costume taped solidly together, tape the white paper heart you made in Step 2 over the front panel of the heart and cut out the 12" × 12" (30.5 × 30.5 cm) window for the face hole.

Decorating and Finishing

8 Wrap the sides and back of the heart with red wrapping paper. When wrapping the heart around the sides, make sure you have enough width; allow an extra 4" (10 cm) of paper to wrap around the front edges of the heart box, all the way down to the white paper heart.

9 From the three sheets of black paper, cut the following: seven 6" × 9" (15 × 23 cm) rectangles; four 8" (20.3 cm) diameter circles; and twelve 2" × 24" (5 × 61 cm) strips of black paper.

10 Fan-fold a 2" × 24" (5 × 61 cm) strip of black paper by folding it back and forth in 2" (5 cm) wide folds. Do this for all 12 strips. They will be the papers around the candies.

11 Tape fan-folded black paper strips around the outside of each 6" × 9" (15 × 23 cm) black paper square and 8" (20.3 cm) diameter circle. These circles and squares will be the candy wrappers. Tape one fan-folded paper around the face window opening also.

12 Glue each candy wrapper onto the front of the heart box.

13 Paint all 5" × 8" (12.5 × 20.3 cm) blocks of foam with brown acrylic paint. Let dry. Glue the blocks into their wrappers.

14 Paint the 8" (20.3 cm) circles of foam with acrylic paint; make 2 red and 2 orange. Let dry. Glue the foam circles into the round candy wrappers.

15 Using hot pink, red, and green acrylic paint mixed with gel medium to add thickness, decorate the "candies" with heart shapes, curlicues, zigzags, and roses with stems (see photo). Let dry.

Who wouldn't want to be a big sweetheart?

Hot Air Balloon

MATERIALS

- round wire tomato tower (trellis)
- 20" (51 cm) diameter inflatable beach ball
- round wicker or plastic basket 12" to 15" (30.5 to 38 cm) tall × 20" (51 cm) diameter*
- duct tape
- clear tape
- roll of twine
- four pink preassembled ribbon bows
- four yellow preassembled ribbon bows
- spool of curly orange ribbon
- spool of curly pink ribbon
- four small brown paper bags
- two 36" × 1" (91 × 2.5 cm) lengths of strong ribbon for straps of costume
- 6' (about 2 m) of nylon fishing line
- a few pieces of paper

*Basket should be large enough to fit around child, and basket edges should line up with trellis legs.

TOOLS: diagonal-cutting pliers, saw, pliers, scissors, ruler

CHILD WEARS: white or black pants and shoes. This will keep the color focus on the costume. Cute long-sleeved striped shirt on top. A boy might wear a beanie and a painted-on French mustache. Girl could wear hair pulled back with festive ribbons.

DIRECTIONS

1 Take the tomato trellis and cut the last 2 circles off the frame with diagonal-cutting pliers to assure enough room for the child to stand and move comfortably, but leave the uprights.

2 Cut out the bottom of the basket with the saw. Cut just inside of the frame; don't cut the frame or the basket will fall apart.

3 Tape any rough edges on the tomato trellis with duct tape to make all edges smooth.

4 To attach the tomato trellis to the basket, start by slipping all four upright wire legs from the tomato trellis into the top of the basket. Keep the wires aligned and about a foot (30 cm) apart from each other. Measure down from the second circle on the tomato frame to the top of

Steps 4 and 5. Trellis leg is slipped through basket, bent up, and twisted around itself.

*Up, up, and
away!*

the basket. This distance should be the same on all 4 legs of the trellis to keep the tomato trellis circles parallel to the top of the basket. Put the beach ball in the upper circle of trellis. Adjust the height of the costume so the child can stand in it without the ball hitting her head. Make sure the costume is not top-heavy.

5 Once the height is determined, bend each wire leg through the basket and twist each leg back up and around the wire frame.

6 Duct-tape these four attachments. Make sure all wire ends are covered by tape.

7 Measure out five 36" (91 cm) strands of twine at a time. Tie them in groups of 5 in a knot at the top of the tomato trellis. Wrap the tomato trellis with the twine. Make sure the tomato trellis does not show through. Measure out additional 36" lengths of twine as needed.

8 Open up the pink ribbon bows and tape on the top circle of the tomato trellis, evenly spaced around the top, about 10" (25 cm) apart.

9 Cut about five 18" (45.5 cm) strands of curly orange ribbon and hang these like bunting between the pink bows (see photo).

10 Use yellow ribbon bows and pink curly ribbon for bunting to decorate the lower circle of the tomato trellis, the same way you did in Step 9.

11 Fill the small brown bags with paper. Tie off the top of the bags with twine. These will be the sandbags. Then use twine to tie each bag to one of the four uprights of the trellis.

12 Tie the strong ribbons through the top edge of the basket in front and in back, about 10" (25 cm) apart, to make two shoulder straps that will fit over your child's clothes. Criss-cross straps in back before tying. Have child stand in the basket and adjust the straps to the child's height. Distribute the weight evenly.

13 Place the beach ball in the frame and secure it with a few pieces of nylon fishing line attached to the frame and over the ball.

Lemonade Stand

MATERIALS

- 24" × 36" (61 × 91.5 cm) white foam core board, ¼" (0.6 cm) wide
- 27" × 48" (68.5 × 122 cm) piece of corrugated cardboard
- two 14" × 14" (35.5 × 35.5 cm) pieces of corrugated cardboard (sides)
- 48" (122 cm) strong curly white ribbon for straps, ½" (1.2 cm) wide
- five red paper cups
- two ⅜" (1 cm) diameter 48" (122 cm) wooden dowels
- 4 yards (3.7 m) thin red ribbon
- 28" × 7' (71 × 213 cm) yellow wrapping paper
- roll of 1" (2.5 cm) wide yellow tape
- roll of 2" (5 cm) wide clear packing tape
- tacky glue
- red, light yellow, dark yellow, white, and black acrylic paints
- 20" × 30" (51 × 76 cm) white butcher paper

TOOLS: ¼" (0.5 cm) paintbrush, craft knife, scissors, ruler

CHILD WEARS: blue shirt, pants, and sandals, or goes barefoot

DIRECTIONS

1 Cut a 13" × 27" (33 × 68.4 cm) rectangle of cardboard and cover with white butcher paper for a sign.

2 Paint "Lemonade" across the sign in red paint. Let dry.

3 Cut a 4" × 27" (10 × 68.5 cm) rectangle of cardboard and cover with white butcher paper. It will be the shelf.

4 Cut a 10" × 27" (25.5 × 68.5 cm) rectangle of cardboard and cover with yellow wrapping paper to be the front of the stand.

5 Cut a 14" × 27" (35.5 × 68.5 cm) rectangle of cardboard and wrap one side with yellow wrapping paper. This will be the back wall.

Lemonade 1⁰⁰

When life brings you lemons, make lemonade.

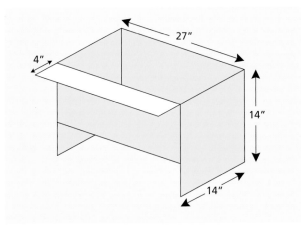

Steps 9 to 11. The stand with its shelf.

6 Take the two 14" × 14" (35.5 × 35.5 cm) squares of cardboard and cover each with yellow wrapping paper.

7 Cover the 2 dowels with white butcher paper by twisting and taping a thin strip of paper around each dowel.

8 Tape the red ribbon at top of dowel and twist it around dowel. Tape at bottom also. Repeat this on the other dowel.

9 Tape the white 4" × 27" (10 × 68.5 cm) shelf panel on its long side to the yellow 10" × 27" (25.5 × 68.5 cm) front panel on its long side, using 2" (5 cm) wide clear tape. The 4" × 27" shelf panel extends out from the front panel.

10 Tape a yellow 14" × 14" (35.5 × 35.5 cm) side panel to each side of the yellow front panel, using 2" (5 cm) clear packing tape.

11 Tape the 14" × 27" (35.5 × 68.5 cm) back wall from Step 5, with its yellow side facing front (inward), to each of the 14" × 14" (35.5 × 35.5 cm) side panels. This should leave you with a rectangular box shape that is open at the bottom and top.

12 Tape a dowel inside each front corner of the box. As much as possible of the dowel should be taped inside the box, so the structure will be strong.

13 Tape the "Lemonade" sign near the top of the dowels.

14 Glue red paper cups to white ledge of the stand.

15 Cut out two 8" (20 cm) diameter circles of foam core board for lemon slices. Cut three whole lemon shapes out of foam core board. Cut out one glass with a lemon slice shape (see photo) out of foam core board.

16 Paint the whole lemon shapes dark yellow. Let dry and tape edges with yellow tape.

17 Paint the lemon slice circles with light yellow. Let dry. Then paint their outer edges with dark yellow paint. Paint 1" (2.5 cm) white lines around the insides (see photo) of the slices for highlights. Let dry. Tape outer edges with yellow tape. Paint the glass of lemonade, straw, and ice cubes as shown in photo. Outline with black paint.

18 Cut one lemon slice circle in half. Tape its cut edges with yellow tape.

19 On one circle, paint "$1.00" or another price.

20 Tape three lemons and two slices with clear tape to the stand (see photo).

21 Paint and tape the lemonade glass shape and the circle with the price to the top of the sign.

22 Poke a hole on the front of the stand about 9" (23 cm) in from the right corner of the stand and an inch (2.5 cm) down from the counter. Poke another hole about 9" in from the left corner. Do the same on the back of the stand. Take a 48" (122 cm) length of white ribbon and knot it on the outside of the stand. Thread the ribbon through a hole in the front. Do the same with the second length of ribbon. These ribbons will be the straps that rest on the child's shoulders. Criss-cross the ribbons. Tie off the ribbons on the back of the stand, after adjusting the straps to your child's height.

Lobster

Surprise everyone with this leggy costume

MATERIALS

- 2" (5 cm) wide clear packing tape
- fifteen red plastic plates, dinner size
- twenty-four 12 oz (360 mL) red plastic disposable cups*
- four to six pieces of 12" × 12" (30.5 × 30.5 cm) red felt for claws
- 16" × 16" (40.5 × 40.5) red felt for hat
- red tape
- clear packing tape
- 24" × 24" (61 × 61 cm) piece of corrugated cardboard
- 8 oz (240 mL) bottle of white glue
- red thread
- 6 yards (5.5 m) thin wire
- red ribbon, ½" (1.2 cm) wide: 96" (243 cm) to tie on claws, for hat ties, and for straps

*Science buffs may notice that our lobster is missing two legs. Actually, lobsters have 8 legs plus two claws. If you wish, add another two legs, in which case you need 8 more cups and more wire.

TOOLS: scissors, craft knife, ruling compass, wire cutter, hole punch, ruler, sewing needle, straight pins

CHILD WEARS: red sweatshirt, red sweatpants, red tennis shoes

DIRECTIONS

1 For the breastplate, arrange 4 or 5 plates on a table by partially overlapping one on the next in a row, with the backs of the plates up. Use red tape to attach the bottom of the first plate to the top back of the next plate. Repeat this with the rest of the plates. You might need 4 or 5 plates, depending on the child's height. The breastplate should cover the child from the collar to the thighs. Make a second row of plates for the backplate in the same way.

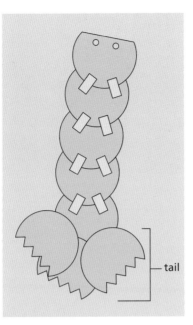

Steps 1 to 3. Assembly of plates to make the breastplate and backplate. Dots at top are holes where ribbons will go. Extra 3 plates for tail are added to the back only.

next cup to the sticky tape. This will help your lobster legs to have shape. Attach 4 cups in total for each leg. Make a total of 6 legs (or 8, if you prefer). Don't trim off the excess wire; you'll need it to attach the legs to the rest of the costume.

5a To attach the legs to the front of the costume, poke 2 holes on the left and 2 on the right side of each of the first 3 plates. Take a leg you made earlier. Thread the loose wire ends through a set of 2 holes, working from the front of the breastplate, and twist the wires together on the back of the breastplate. Cut off the excess wire and tape the wire ends safely in place.

5b To join the front and the back, cut a 24" (61 cm) piece of red ribbon. Tie one end through the left hole in the top plate of the breastplate. Try the costume on the child and tie through the left hole in the top backplate, adjusting length to fit child. Repeat for the right side of the breastplate and backplate.

2 Cut across the first (top) plate of the breastplate about 3" (7.5 cm) down to make a flat top. Tape the cut edge with clear tape to keep it smooth. With a hole punch, punch two holes on the taped edge, about 1" (2.5 cm) in from the edge and 3" (7.5 cm) apart. These holes are for the straps that will go over the child's shoulders. Cut and tape the first (top) plate of the backplate in the same way, and punch 2 holes in the top of the first plate of the backplate also.

3 For the tail, cut a jagged, sawtooth edge across each of 3 plates, about ⅓ of the way up. Tape the 3 sawtooth plates to the lowest plate in the backplate stack you made.

4 There will be 6 legs, 3 on each side (or, if you prefer, make 4 on each side). To make a leg, poke 2 holes about an inch (2.5 cm) apart through the bottom of each of 4 red cups. Cut a 36" (91.5 cm) piece of wire. Fold wire in half. Then slip the ends of the wire in the holes on the bottom of the cup, starting from outside the cup. Twist the wires together in the inside of the cup. Then slip the wires into the holes of the next cup. Make a circle with the tape, leaving the sticky side out, and stick the tape on the inside bottom of the first cup. Press the

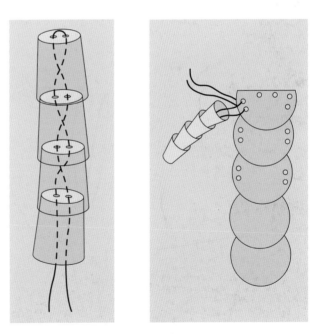

Step 4. Assembling a leg. Twist wires around each other inside each cup before adding the next one.

Step 5a. Leg being attached to side of breastplate by wires.

6 For each lobster claw, cut two 10" (25.5 cm) diameter circles from cardboard. Cut away one-fourth of each circle. Use the remaining three-fourths circle as a pattern to cut four claw shapes of red felt. Fold the remaining three-fourths cardboard circle in half, and glue the felt claw shapes on its front and back. Punch holes about 3" (7.5 cm) apart on each, near the fold (see diagram). Cut two 12" (30.5 cm) long red ribbons. Pull a red ribbon through the holes on one claw. Tie it around the child's wrists. Repeat for second claw.

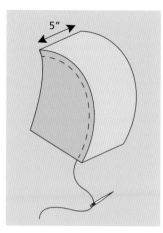

Step 6. A three-quarters circle becomes a claw when it is bent.

Step 7. For the hat, stitch the straight 5" x 14" (12.7 x 35.5 cm) strip of felt to each side piece.

Hat

7 To make the hat, cut the following from the 16" × 16" (40.5 × 40.5 cm) piece of red felt: 5" × 14" (12.7 × 35.5 cm) strip, two 7" × 8" (17.8 × 20.3 cm) pieces, and two 1" × 12" (2.5 × 30.5 cm) strips. To make the hat sides, round one corner of each of the 7" × 8" hat side pieces by trimming away a corner. With needle and thread, sew the long edge of the 5" × 14" strip around the edge of each 7" × 8" hat side piece of felt on the two rounded sides, with about ¼" (6 mm) seam allowance. Turn right-side out so seams are inside.

8 Fold the 1" × 12" (2.5 × 30.5 cm) strips in half so the width is ½" × 12" (1.2 × 30.5 cm), pin, and sew up the short edge and the long edge. Turn right-side out. This will make one antenna. Repeat to make a second antenna. Stitch antennae to top of hat.

9 Cut two 12" (30.5 cm) pieces of red ribbon for ties, and sew a ribbon tie to each of the corners of the hat that will be near the child's chin, if desired.

Octopus

MATERIALS

- 16" (40 cm) string
- two 23" × 25" (58.5 × 63.5 cm) pieces of corrugated cardboard
- 24" × 24" (61 × 61 cm) piece of corrugated cardboard
- plastic purple tablecloth
- two hundred ¾ oz (22 mL) plastic soufflé cups (used in take-out restaurants for salad dressing)
- sixty-four 8 oz (240 mL) plastic purple drinking cups
- 5 oz (148 mL) tacky glue
- roll of 2" (5 cm) wide clear packing tape
- two white 8" (20 cm) plastic plates
- two 16 oz (480 mL) black plastic cups
- eight 48" (122 cm) long wires

TOOLS: pushpin, craft knife, scissors, wire cutters, pencil, ruler

CHILD WEARS: purple or black long-sleeved shirt, black pants, and black shoes, or all white

DIRECTIONS

Making the Shoulder Circle

1 To make the shoulder circle, draw a circle of radius 12" (30.5 cm) on the 24" × 24" (61 × 61 cm) cardboard (diameter of circle will be 24"). To do this, draw diagonal lines on the cardboard, connecting both corners to make an "X" in order to find the center. To draw the circle,

get a piece of string and stick the pushpin into one end of the string and then into the center point of the cardboard. Tie the other end of the string to a pencil, making sure the string length is exactly 12" (30.5 cm) from the pin. Hold the pin down with one hand. With other hand, bring pencil right to the edge (string should be taut) and swing an arc around the cardboard so the pencil marks a circle. Adjust the string to 4" (10 cm) long and mark another circle of 4" radius, keeping the pin in the center. Diameter will be 8" (20 cm). You will have drawn a doughnut shape on your cardboard.

2 With a craft knife, cut the 24" (61 cm) diameter shoulder circle out of the cardboard. Cut out the center 8" (20 cm) diameter circle also.

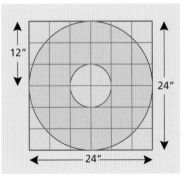

Steps 1 and 2. Pattern for shoulder circle. 1 box = 4" (10 cm). Gray parts are cut away.

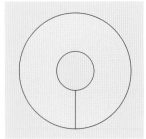

Step 3. Cut a slit in shoulder circle so wearer can get into and out of costume.

3 Make a straight slit through the cardboard from the inner circle to the outer circle. Cover one side of the shoulder circle with a piece of purple plastic tablecloth, using the tape to secure it. Slit open the plastic over the cardboard slit, so the child can get in and out easily. Cut away the plastic over the inner circle and tape any ends in place.

Making and Attaching Legs

4 Fold each of the eight 48" (122 cm) wires in half.

5 Take the sixty-four 8" (20 cm) purple plastic cups and poke two holes at the bottom of each cup, about 1" (2.5 cm) apart. Put the ends of one wire into each of the holes at the bottom of a cup, starting from the outside. Inside the cup, twist the two wire ends together twice. Slip another cup onto the wire so it looks as though you are stacking the cups. Keep adding cups until you have a strand of 8 cups. That will be one leg. Don't cut off the extra wire. Make the other 7 legs the same way.

6 You can use packing tape inside of the cups that make up the legs to hold the legs in whatever position you want.

7 To attach the suckers, lay all legs on the table. Place 200 soufflé cups upside down and tacky-glue the bottoms. Let the tacky glue set for a few minutes. Then take some soufflé cups and place 20 to 25 on one of the 8 arms, bottoms down. Attach the cups side by side in rows to look like the suction cups of an octopus. Do this to all 8 legs. Let the legs dry overnight.

8 To attach the legs to the shoulder circle, poke two holes that are 2" (5 cm) apart near the outer edge of the shoulder circle that you cut out earlier. Turn the shoulder circle purple-side down. Put the wires from one leg up through the holes, twisting them together tightly and taping the wire down on the upper (uncovered) side of the circle. Make sure the last cup that makes up the leg is flush against the covered underside of the shoulder circle. Spacing the remaining 7 legs evenly around the shoulder circle, attach them in the same way. Cut off any excess wire.

9 Once all the legs are attached to the shoulder circle, cover the top side of the circle with part of the purple plastic tablecloth. Cut a slit in the plastic over the slit in the cardboard. Trim off the unused plastic that extends beyond the edges and cut away the excess tablecloth in the center, close to the inside edge of the inner circle. Tape down any loose edges.

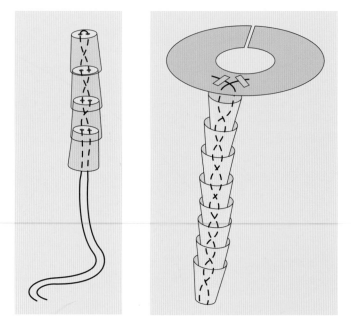

Step 5. Assembling a leg. Twist wires around each other inside each cup before adding the next one.

Step 8. Leg attached to underside of shoulder circle; wire ends twisted together and taped in place on top.

Always ready to lend a hand.

Making the Head

10 On a 23" × 25" (58.5 × 63.5 cm) piece of cardboard, draw a petal shape that tapers to be 12" (30 cm) across at the face end (see diagram). Cut the shape out and trace and cut out the same shape on another 23" × 25" piece of cardboard.

11 Tape these two petal shapes together, one on top of the other, to create the octopus's head. At the narrow end of the shape, we need to cut out an upside-down "U" that is about 9" wide × 5" tall (23 × 12.5 cm) for the face opening. Measure your child's head before cutting to be sure this octopus head will fit well, and adjust the opening size to your child's face.

12 Cover the whole cardboard head with purple plastic tablecloth, trimming the plastic to shape and taping and gluing edges down.

13 For the eyes, glue two white plates side by side above the face opening. Cut down two black cups to be 2" (5 cm) tall and glue them, with the bottoms facing up, on top of the white plates to finish the eyes. Try the hat on the child; add strings to hold it on if necessary.

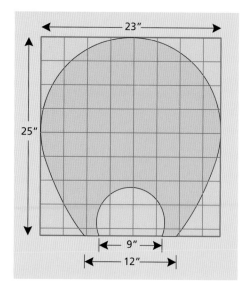

Step 10. Pattern for head. 1 box = 3" (7.5 cm). Gray parts are cut away.

Paper Airplane

MATERIALS

- eight 15" × 96" (38 × 244 cm) pieces of white butcher paper
- four 34" × 50" (86 × 127 cm) pieces of corrugated cardboard or two 64" × 50" (163 × 127 cm) pieces
- roll of 2" (5 cm) wide clear packing tape
- 2 oz (56 g) white glue
- two 72" (182 cm) lengths of strong white 1" (2.5 cm) wide ribbon for straps
- 8½" × 11" (21.5 × 28 cm) white paper for hat
- two 18" (46 cm) pieces of thin cord to tie on paper hat

TOOLS: scissors, craft knife, pencil, yardstick

CHILD WEARS: clothes that contrast with paper

DIRECTIONS

1 Lay the four 15" × 96" (38 × 244 cm) pieces of butcher paper side by side on their long sides and tape together, using 2" (5 cm) wide clear packing tape. This gives you a large piece of paper, 60" × 96" (152.4 × 244 cm).

2 Fold this sheet in half so that you have a folded piece of paper that is 60" × 48" (152.4 × 122 cm). This first fold line is the spine of the airplane.

3a Open up fold and align paper so the first fold runs from left to right on the table. Then take the lower left corner and fold up so what was the paper's left edge aligns with the spine.

3b Repeat with the upper left corner, folding it in and aligning its former left edge with the spine. This leaves a point at the end of a triangular shape on the left side of the paper. This point will be the front of the airplane.

4 Now re-crease the spine so its fold is sharp.

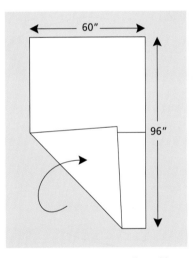

Step 3a. Fold corner up to align with spine fold.

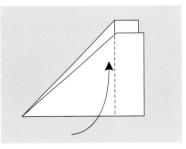

Step 4. Re-crease spine.

Check out this flight suit!

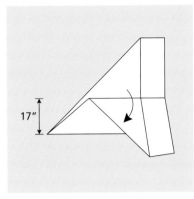

Step 5a. Measure up 17" (43 cm) from spine, and fold wing down.

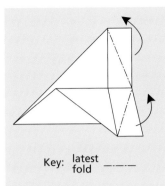

Key: latest fold ─·─·─

Step 5b. Fold up back corners of wings.

7 Arrange the 34" × 50" (86 × 127 cm) cardboards together to be larger in area than the spread-out plane. Overlap the cardboard sections 2" (5 cm) on each other and tape them together, using 2" (5 cm) wide clear packing tape. Don't overlap the cardboards at the spine, however; just tape the upper and lower boards right next to each other there. Using the spread-out airplane as your template, cut two joined wing shapes from cardboard, tracing the shape of the wings from the plane (see diagram), but not including the folded-up back corners from Step 5b. The spine is the dividing line between the two wing shapes.

8 Piece together four 15" × 96" (38 × 244 cm) pieces of white butcher paper on their long sides and wrap the cardboard shape you just cut in the butcher paper, cutting off excess and taping paper in place. Insert the wrapped cardboard plane shape in the paper plane, using glue to attach it to the paper airplane. Refold plane.

5a Measure up 17" (43 cm), about one-third the way up from the spine, and fold the wing nearest you down towards the spine, making sure the crease of the wing fold is parallel to the spine. Fold the wing on the other side of the plane down in the same way.

5b Fold the back corners up from the end of the overlapped paper to the 17" (43 cm) line (see diagram).

6 Spread out the spine and wing folds so you see a flattened, almost triangular plane shape. Set aside.

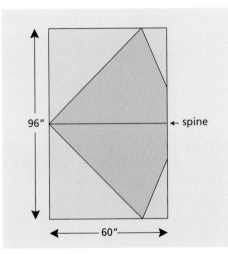

Step 7. Cut cardboard shape same size as flattened plane. 1 box = 12" (30.5 cm). Gray areas are cut away.

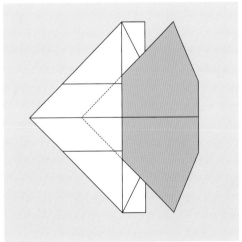

Step 8. Insert wrapped cardboard into the paper plane made in Step 5.

9 Draw a 12" (30.5 cm) diameter circle, centered on the airplane's spine, about 32" (81 cm) back from the nose point of the airplane. Extend this into an oval shape 12" × 48" (30.5 × 122 cm). This oval will be the place in which the child will stand. Cut away the oval from the paper and cardboard. Try the costume on the child to be sure he has room to stand; widen oval if needed. Use 2" wide (5 cm) clear packing tape to tape down the paper around the hole to get clean lines. While the child is still in the costume, mark the position of two holes in front of the oval and two in back of the oval on the wings, to position the straps.

10 Have the child take off the airplane. Poke the strap holes through the paper and cardboard. Feed the ribbons through the holes and tie them on. Adjust their length to child.

11 When the costume is refolded into the airplane shape and the child is wearing costume, you can tape the two halves together above the spine in the rear and middle of the plane, so that the costume will hold its shape.

12 Cutting the oval through the spine weakens the airplane, making it tend to droop in the back. You can fix this by taping a small card-board box to the spine of the airplane for support against the back of the child. Do this while fitting the costume to be certain of the best effect. Turn the wing tips up as in photo.

13 Make a little paper airplane in the same way from an 8½" × 11" (21.5 × 28 cm) piece of paper. Punch two holes in it for strings and tie it on for a hat.

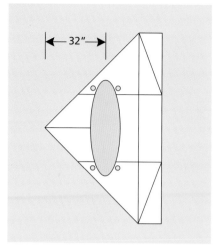

Steps 9 and 10. Make oval cutout so child can wear costume. Small dots indicate holes for ribbons.

A group of friends in their costumes.

Pencil

MATERIALS

- 24" × 48" (61 × 122 cm) piece of corrugated cardboard
- 20" × 54" (51 × 137 cm) piece of corrugated cardboard
- 14" × 14" (35.5 × 35.5 cm) piece of corrugated cardboard
- 12" × 30" (30.5 × 76 cm) piece of corrugated cardboard
- 11" × 54" (28 × 137 cm) polyurethane foam, ½" (1.2 cm) thick
- 2" (5 cm) wide clear packing tape
- ½" (1.2 cm) wide black tape
- 13" × 56" (33 × 142 cm) piece of pink cotton knit (T-shirt material)
- 48" × 24" (122 × 61 cm) yellow wrapping paper
- 10" × 54" (25.5 × 137 cm) silver Mylar sheet or duct tape
- two large brown paper bags

TOOLS: craft knife, scissors, yardstick or long ruler, pencil, hot glue gun

CHILD WEARS: neutral or dark-colored pants, shirt, shoes

DIRECTIONS

1 Take the 24" × 48" (61 × 122 cm) corrugated cardboard and mark and crease every 8" (20 cm) on the 48" (122 cm) side. Tape the 24" sides together to make a six-sided tube.

2 Lay down a piece of 14" × 14" (35.5 × 35.5 cm) cardboard. Stand your six-sided tube on top of the cardboard and trace around the bottom hexagon shape.

3 Cut out the traced hexagon and tape it on the top of the cardboard tube.

4 Cut six 2" × 30" (5 × 76 cm) strips of corrugated cardboard from the 12" × 30" (30.5 × 76 cm) piece. Fold the strips in half and tape these in a teepee shape around the top of the tube to form a point (see diagram). The strips will overlap each other.

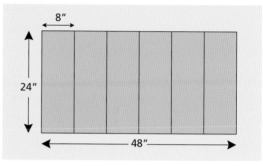

Step 1. Rule and crease lines as shown.

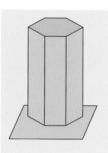

Step 2. Trace around hexagonal tube to make the top for the pencil.

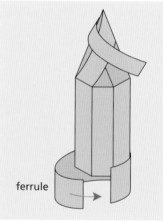

Steps 4 to 6. Folded strips of cardboard form the point. A rounded strip of cardboard, partly overlapping the hexagonal tube, forms the ferrule.

5 Fill in open spots in between the cardboard strips with more cardboard. Tape and fit the pieces together smoothly.

6 To make the ferrule (the "metal" part), cut an 8" × 52" (20 × 132 cm) rectangle of corrugated cardboard from the 20" × 54" (51 × 137 cm) piece. Bend and tape it securely to the open end of the tube with clear tape, overlapping the cardboard at least 1" (2.5 cm) over the end of the tube.

*Pencil
me in.*

7 For an eraser, cut an 11" × 54" (28 × 137 cm) rectangle of cardboard. Bend and tape it below the ferrule you just attached. Let the new cardboard overlap the end of the ferrule at least 1" (2.5 cm).

8 Take an 11" × 54" (28 × 137 cm) piece of polyurethane foam. Using hot glue, cover the foam with pink T-shirt material, folding the excess material around to cover the edges of the foam. Then hot-glue the pink-covered foam all the way around the part of the cardboard you are using as an eraser, tucking in and gluing under any loose edges.

9 To fit the costume to the child, have the child hold the costume; mark a small hole where you think the child's face will be when he is wearing the costume. Remove the costume and cut the hole for the child's face. Then place the cylinder over the child's head to figure out where to cut out the final holes for the face and arms. Look in the peephole you cut in the costume, and use a pencil to draw a circle on the outside of the tube that is about the size of the child's face. Also try to find out where you want the armholes to be, and trace the circles that you will cut out for them. Remove the costume and cut out the circles.

10 Cut open the two brown paper bags and make 3" (7.5 cm) wide strips from it. Wrap the point of the cylinder with the strips, taping and gluing them on. This will be the tip of pencil.

11 Now cover the main 24" × 48" (61 × 122 cm) barrel of the pencil with yellow wrapping paper, up to the ferrule, overlapping the brown paper point with yellow paper by 5" (12.5 cm). Tape and secure the yellow paper to the cylinder on the sides, and scallop (cut curved edges, as seen in photo) the overlapping yellow paper on the top, taping the yellow paper to the brown paper to make the pencil look as though it has been sharpened.

12 Take the 10" × 54" (25.5 × 137 cm) silver Mylar sheet and adhere it to the costume on the ferrule, overlapping the pink eraser on one side and the yellow wrapping paper on the other. Circle the entire cylinder with Mylar. If you don't have Mylar, you can use duct tape.

13 Cover each edge of the Mylar with thin black tape.

14 Wrap the point of the pencil with 6" (15 cm) of black tape to make a "lead" for the pencil.

Piggy Bank

MATERIALS

- pushpin
- string 30" (76 cm) long
- five 24" × 48" (61 × 122 cm) pieces of corrugated cardboard
- 15' × 28" (4.6 m × 71 cm) pink wrapping paper
- 2" (5 cm) wide roll clear packing tape
- three 8" × 12" (20 × 30.5 cm) pieces of pink felt
- black acrylic paint
- gold-colored cardboard cake plate
- plastic headband
- glue

TOOLS: paintbrush, craft knife, scissors, ruler, pencil

CHILD WEARS: pink top under costume and cute shoes, dark pants

DIRECTIONS

1 On the first 24" × 48" (61 × 122 cm) cardboard, draw and cut out two 24" (61 cm) diameter circles (radius 12" or 30.5 cm). See page 53 for general instructions on drawing circles.

2 Bend the spine of a second 24" × 48" (61 × 122 cm) piece of cardboard to shape it into a cylinder, and tape one 48" edge to a 24" circle, using 2" (5 cm) wide clear tape. Tape the other 24" circle to the other cylinder end. This makes the body of the piggy bank. On what will become the top center of this cylinder, cut a round hole big enough for the child's head. About 6" (15 cm) to one side of the hole, make a 2" × 10" (5 × 25 cm) coin slot. Below it, on the opposite side of the cylinder, cut a space big

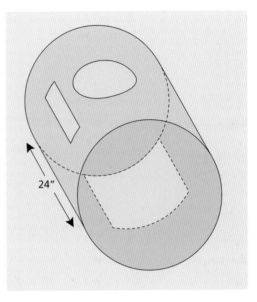

Step 2. Body cylinder has cutouts for child's head, legs, and a coin slot (gray areas).

enough for the child to stand. Try the costume on the child to be sure it fits well.

3 From the third 24" × 48" (61 × 122 cm) cardboard, cut two 7" × 48" (18 × 122 cm) strips (one for the head and one for the snout), a 10" (25 cm) diameter circle for the head, and four 8" (20.3 cm) diameter circles for feet.

4 From the fourth 24" × 48" cardboard, cut four 5" × 48" (12.7 × 122 cm) strips for feet.

5 From the fifth 24" × 48" cardboard, cut an 18" (45.5 cm) diameter circle to create the head of the pig. Save the rest for later.

6 For each of the 7" × 48" (18 × 122 cm) strips of cardboard, bend and break down the spine of the cardboard. Tape one 7" × 48" strip on its

See what saving money can do?

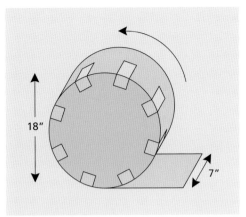

Step 6. Tape a strip on the 18" (45.5 cm) diameter circle as shown.

long side to the 18" (45.5 cm) circle to create the head of the pig. Use part of the next 7" (18 cm) wide strip to complete the head.

7 For the snout, in the same way, tape the rest of the 7" × 48" (18 × 122 cm) cardboard strip to the 10" (25.5 cm) diameter circle until the ends meet; cut off any excess from the strip.

8 For the feet, take the four 5" × 48" (12.5 × 122 cm) cardboard strips. In the same way as for the head of the pig, break the spine of the cardboard and tape one long side around each 8" (20 cm) diameter circle until the ends meet; cut off the excess strip.

9 Wrap each pig piece with pink wrapping paper. The easiest way is to measure, wrap, and tape the paper around the cylinders and cut out the circles separately. Tape the circles on the fronts of the cylinders.

10 Once everything is wrapped with pink paper, tape the head (18" or 45.5 cm diameter), centered on the body cylinder's front, as shown in the photo.

11 Tape on the snout (10" or 25.5 cm cylinder), centered on the front of the head, as shown in the photo.

12 Tape the feet on the underside of the pig (see photo).

13 For ears, cut two 8" (20 cm) triangles from cardboard. Cover with pink wrapping paper on outside and pink felt on the inside. Tape ears to top of the head.

14 Cut four 2" × 8" (5 × 20 cm) strips of pink felt, and cut a "V" in the center of each strip on one long side. Glue one strip on the front of each of the pig's feet for a hoof.

15 With black paint, paint on eyes and nostrils as shown in the photo.

16 Paint the number "25" on the gold cake plate. Let dry. Tape the cake plate to the head-band with clear tape.

Popcorn

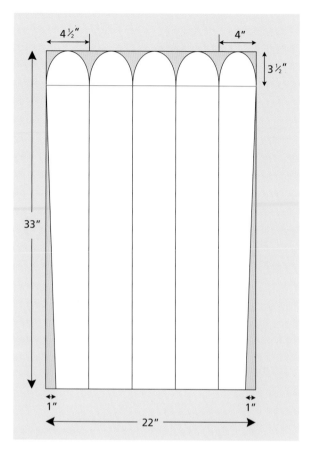

Steps 2 to 4. Pattern for side of popcorn container. 1 box = 3" (7.5 cm). Cut away excess above scallops and taper sides as shown (gray areas).

MATERIALS

- 48" × 96" (122 × 244 cm) white foam core board, ¼" (0.5 cm) thick
- 22" × 22" (56 × 56 cm) square of foam core board for top
- pencil
- 6 oz (180 mL) red acrylic paint
- black marker
- roll of 1" (2.5 cm) wide white tape
- roll of 1" (2.5 cm) wide red tape
- roll of 2" (5 cm) wide clear packing tape
- roll of masking tape
- 24" × 36" (61 × 91.5 cm) yellow construction paper
- 24" × 36" (61 × 91.5 cm) black construction paper
- 24 oz (720 mL) bag of Styrofoam packing popcorn
- yellow baseball cap
- glue

TOOLS: ruling compass, craft knife, yardstick or long ruler, narrow (¼" or 6 mm) paintbrush, hot glue gun, and narrow cotton paint roller for the stripes

CHILD WEARS: whatever she prefers under costume, since most of her clothes will not show, but cute shoes and bright-colored socks

DIRECTIONS

1 Cut foam core board down to 33" × 88" (84 × 223.5 cm). Divide board into four pieces that are 22" × 33" (56 × 84 cm) each. These will be the sides of the container.

2 On one short end of each 22" × 33" board, mark down 3½" (9 cm). Draw a line across the 22" width at 3½". Repeat on all four pieces.

3 Divide the line you just drew into four 4½" (11.4 cm) wide segments and one segment that is 4" (10 cm) wide. With a compass, mark scallops above the line. You should have five scallops. Cut away the board above the scallops with a craft knife. Repeat this on the tops of the other three 22" × 33" (56 × 84 cm) pieces of foam core board.

4 With a pencil, mark a short line 1" (2.5 cm) in from each side at the bottom of each 22" × 33" (56 × 84 cm) board. Then align the yardstick from the top corner on the right side to the 1" (2.5 cm) mark on the bottom right and draw the line between to taper the side. Cut off the excess with the craft knife. Repeat on the left side. Taper each of the three remaining 22" ×

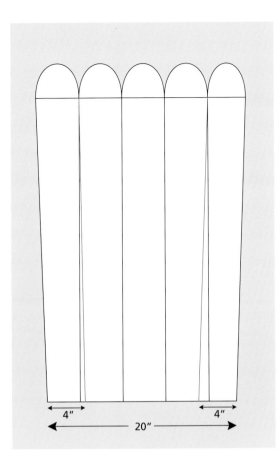

Step 5. Angle the paint lines of side sections as shown (red lines).

Got butter?

33" sides the same way. Each side section should now be 20" (51 cm) at the bottom; the top should have 5 scallops.

5 On the 20" (50.8 cm) edge of each container side, measure in 4" (10 cm) from each of the two outer edges and make a small mark. With a yardstick, draw a line from each mark you just made to the corresponding mark at the lowest point between the first and second and fourth and fifth scallops on the top edge (see diagram). Repeat this on each board. These new lines are the paint lines for the outer sections.

6 Lay one of the 20" × 33" (50.8 × 84 cm) sides of the box on a work table. Run a strip of masking tape on the sides of each area where a red stripe will go. This will keep any excess paint from getting on the sections that are supposed to be white. Use the narrow cotton roller to paint the red sections. See photo; colors alternate. Two box sections start and end with red, and two start and end with white. Prepare and paint all three remaining 20" × 33" panels. Let paint dry. Then gently remove the masking tape.

7 Place all four side sections on the floor, face down. Join the sides together with tape on the long sides, making a box shape, taping on the unpainted side of the boards so the container ends up straight when standing upright.

8 Take the 22" × 22" (56 × 56 cm) square of foam core board, and cut a circle out of the center big enough for your child's head to go through. Tape this square inside the assembled popcorn box, just below the scallops.

9 With your red tape, cover the top edges of all the red scallops. With your white tape, cover the top edges of all the white scallops. Cover the seams where the sides meet on the outside with either red or white tape, whichever matches best.

10 On a piece of yellow paper, draw letters saying POPCORN. Cut out the letters and trace around them on the black paper. Cut out the letters from the black paper. Glue the letters to the popcorn box with the yellow letters partly overlapping the black ones (see photo).

11 Hot-glue little Styrofoam popcorn pieces all over the baseball cap.

12 Have the child stand in the costume and fill the top with Styrofoam packing popcorn.

Race Car

MATERIALS

- 14" × 3" (35.5 × 7.5 cm) piece of corrugated cardboard (front, headlights)
- two 36.5" × 9" (93 × 23 cm) pieces of corrugated cardboard (for sides)
- 9" × 20" (23 × 51 cm) piece of corrugated cardboard (rear panel)
- 36" × 20" (91.5 × 51 cm) piece of corrugated cardboard (top panel)
- 8" × 20" (20.3 × 51 cm) piece of corrugated cardboard (spoiler)
- two 8" × 8" (20.3 × 20.3 cm) pieces of corrugated cardboard (pylons for spoiler)
- two 6" × 8" (15.2 × 20.3 cm) pieces of cardboard (fins for spoiler)
- 28" × 2' (71 × 61 cm) black wrapping paper
- 28" × 5' (71 × 153 cm) red wrapping paper
- four disposable round covered Styrofoam containers, about 8" (20 cm) across (for wheels)
- eight 12 oz (360 mL) black plastic cups
- ½" (1.2 cm) wide roll of black tape
- black acrylic paint
- white acrylic paint
- ½" (1.2 cm) diameter × 28" (71 cm) wooden dowel
- ½" (1.2 cm) diameter × 33" (84 cm) wooden dowel
- 24" × 24" (61 × 61 cm) sheet of silver stick-on Mylar
- 2" (5 cm) wide roll clear packing tape
- tacky glue
- 1" × 48" (2.5 × 122 cm) piece of black ribbon
- 12" × 18" (30.5 × 46 cm) black construction paper
- 12" × 18" (30.5 × 46 cm) white construction paper

TOOLS: black marker, pencil, long ruler, craft knife, scissors, paintbrush, ruling compass

CHILD WEARS: white shirt, black pants, and black shoes

DIRECTIONS

For layout of all lines, use a long ruler and a pencil. Refer to the diagrams as you rule and cut the pieces to shape with a craft knife.

Top of Car

1 To lay out the top panel of the car, take the 36" × 20" (91.5 × 51 cm) cardboard and lay it on the work surface so that one longer edge is closest to you. Then:

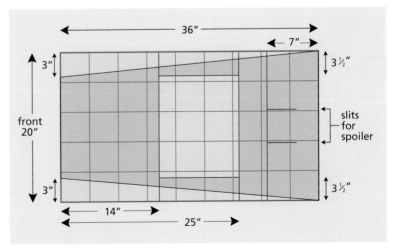

Step 1. Pattern for top of race car. 1 box = 4" (10 cm). Cut away gray parts.

Gentlemen, start your engines!

1a Lay out the points and lines indicated in the Step 1 diagram. The front of the car is at the left in this diagram.

1b Cut along the angled lines to cut away the excess from the cardboard, and cut away the 11" × 13" (28 × 33 cm) rectangle that is in the center of the panel, where the child will stand.

1c Use the craft knife to cut 4" (10 cm) long slits, which later will hold the pylons for the spoiler near the back. The slits start 7" (18 cm) in from the back edge (see diagram). Make sure not to cut all the way out to the edge. You should leave 3" (7.5 cm) uncut at the edge of the panel. Set the top aside for now.

Side Panel

2 To shape the side panel, lay a 36½" × 9" (93 × 23 cm) cardboard on your work surface with a long side closest to you. Rule the side panel as shown in the diagram for Step 2. Repeat this procedure for the second side panel. Cut away the excess part of the side panels as shown.

3 With clear tape, attach the front (14" × 3" or 35.5 × 7.5 cm) and rear panels (9" × 20" or 23 × 51 cm) to the side panels. Then tape on the top panel with 2" (5 cm) wide clear packing tape to complete assembly of the frame for the car (see diagram).

4 Wrap the frame of the car with red wrapping paper, using the 2" (5 cm) clear packing tape to tape inside the frame, taking care to keep clean lines on the car.

5 Mark and cut out holes for the ribbon straps near the corners of the center cutout. Cut the ribbon into two pieces, tie each in front, criss-cross them, and tie each in place at the back of the cutout.

6 Cut all eight 12 oz (360 mL) black plastic cups down to 2" (5 cm) height. These will be used as the headlights on the front panel and as hubcap centers.

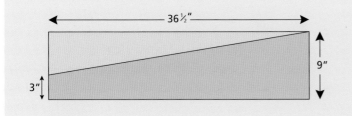

Step 2. Pattern for side panel of car. 1 box = 4" (10 cm). Cut away gray parts.

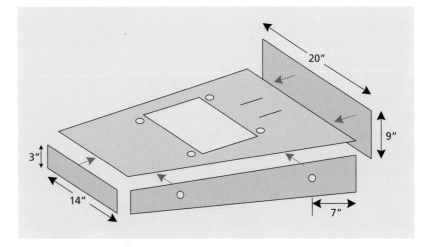

Step 3. Assembling the parts of the car body. Small dots indicate holes for axles and straps.

7 Cut eight 1½" (4 cm) diameter circles out of the sheet of Mylar. Pull off the paper protecting the sticky surface of the Mylar circles and stick them to the headlights and hubcap centers (the bottoms of the black plastic cups).

8 Draw and cut out four 7" (18 cm) diameter circles from the Mylar. Inside each 7" Mylar circle, draw another circle that is 4" (10 cm) in diameter and cut it out, leaving a Mylar donut that is 1½" thick (4 cm). This donut will be used as a decoration on the tires.

9 Paint all of the round disposable containers (which will be wheels) with the black acrylic paint. Let dry.

10 Mix black and white and paint a gray 6" (15 cm) diameter circle in the center of one side of a disposable container (choose either the top or the bottom of the container). Let dry. These will represent the hubcaps of the wheels.

11 Tape black tape around the edges of the round 8" (20 cm) Styrofoam containers where the lid and base meet.

12 Lay the 7" Mylar donuts cut in Step 8 on the wheels over the place where the gray and black paint meet.

13 Tacky-glue four 2" (5 cm) black cups (from Step 6) to the front panel of the car to act as headlights. Use black tape on the headlights where they meet the front panel to create clean lines.

14 For the rear axle, cut ½" (1.2 cm) diameter holes that are 7" (18 cm) in from the rear edge and 2½" (6.3 cm) up from the bottom on both sides of the car (see diagram with Step 3). Feed the longer (33") dowel through both rear holes until the dowel is centered in the car. Repeat this for the front axle, using the 28" (71 cm) dowel and measuring back 7" (18 cm) from the front of the car and up 2½" (6.3 cm).

15 Cut a ½" (1.2 cm) hole in the center of each of the Styrofoam container wheels, cutting the container and lid. Slip each wheel onto one of

the dowels, having some of the dowel protrude. Tacky-glue a 2" (5 cm) black cup onto the center of each wheel, over the dowel.

Decorations

16 Cut the decorative ovals used for the race car from the construction paper, as follows:

For Small Ovals:
- two 5½" × 6" (14 × 15 cm) black ovals
- two 4½" × 5½" (11.4 × 14 cm) white ovals
- two 3¼" × 3½" (8.25 × 9 cm) black #3's

For Large Oval:
- 10" × 12½" (25.5 × 32 cm) black oval
- 8½" × 10" (21.5 × 25.5 cm) white oval
- 6" × 6" (15 × 15 cm) black #3

To assemble the number ovals, glue the small white ovals on the small black ovals. Then glue the small numbers on the white ovals. Do the same for the large oval. Glue the small ovals to each side of the car, and glue the large oval to the hood.

17 To mount the spoiler, you will need to make two pylons. To make each pylon:

17a Measure and rule up the 8" × 8" (20.3 × 20.3 cm) cardboard as shown in the diagram. Cut out the pylon.

17b On the left edge of the pylon, mark a point that is about ¾" (2 cm) up from the bottom. Use the scissors to cut a slit 2" (5 cm) across, parallel to the bottom edge, starting from this mark on the pylon.

17c Wrap the pylon in black wrapping paper, using black tape to create clean lines.

18 Make two triangular fins for the spoiler from 6" × 8" (15.2 × 20.3 cm) cardboard pieces (see diagram). Wrap both fins in black wrapping paper and use black tape to secure it with clean lines.

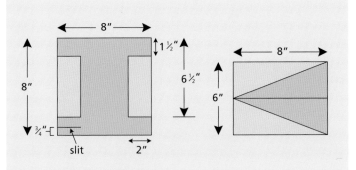

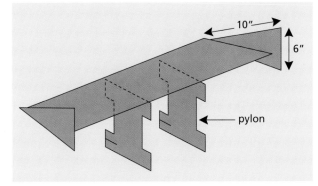

Steps 17 and 18. Left, pattern for pylon. Right, pattern for fin. 1 box = 2" (5 cm). Cut away gray parts.

Step 21. Pylons with spoiler and fins attached.

19 Wrap the 8" × 20" (20 × 51 cm) cardboard panel for the spoiler with black wrapping paper, using black tape to hold it with clean lines. Tape the spoiler to the pylons and tape the fins to the spoiler with black tape.

20 Use the craft knife to feel for 4" (10 cm) pylon slits at the back of the car top, and cut the wrapping paper

there. Do the same to find and cut a slit in the paper over the slit at the bottom of each pylon.

21 Slip each pylon into its slit on the car top and slide it forward until the slit on the bottom of the pylon overlaps the frame of the car and the pylon is seated properly.

Reduced pattern for ovals.

Snowflake

MATERIALS

- 48" × 48" (122 × 122 cm) foam core board, ¼" (0.6 cm) thick
- four rolls of ½" (1.2 cm) wide white tape
- 3 oz (90 mL) white acrylic paint
- 12 oz (360 mL) crystal clear glitter
- 4½ oz (135 mL) silver glitter
- 3 oz (90 mL) blue glitter
- white glue
- two 36" (91.5 cm) pieces of strong white ribbon for straps

TOOLS: craft knife, scissors, ruler, pen, pencil, 3" (7.5 cm) wide cotton roller

CHILD WEARS: all white, or light blue or gray sweatshirt and pants

DIRECTIONS

1 Copy the snowflake pattern on the foam core board. Make sure the pattern touches each edge of the board at its widest point.

2 Trace around the edges of the snowflake with pen.

3 Draw the inside designs (where the glitter will be) with pencil (see photo).

4 Cut the snowflake out of the foam core board with a craft knife. Cut out a 9" wide × 12" long (23 × 30.5 cm) oval right in the center of the snowflake. The oval will be a space for the child's face.

5 Tape with white ½" (1.2 cm) wide tape all the way around the outside edge of snowflake. Tape around the oval's edge also.

6 Place the snowflake flat on your work table where it will dry. With the 3" (7.5 cm) roller, roll white acrylic paint across the face (front) of the

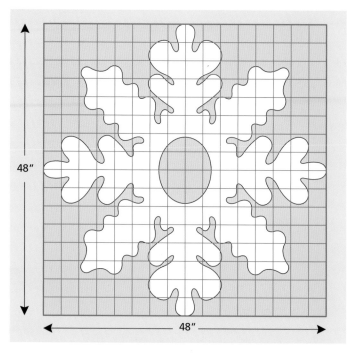

Step 1. Pattern for Snowflake. 1 box = 3" (7.5 cm). Cut away gray parts.

entire snowflake. Let dry. Then roll glue across the face of the snowflake and completely the cover face of the snowflake with crystal clear glitter. Let dry (takes about 2 hours).

7 Dump off the glitter that doesn't stick. With the bottle of white glue, trace around the inside designs, applying glue heavily. Sprinkle silver glitter on the areas you just glued.

8 Take the bottle of glue and highlight the edges of glitter designs you drew (see photo). Sprinkle blue glitter on those areas. Let dry.

9 Have the child hold the snowflake up to her face. Mark a spot near each of her shoulders where a strap can be attached. Poke a hole in the snowflake, and push one ribbon end through to the front and tie there. Tie the long ribbon ends in the back over the child's back, to help support the costume.

Here is a COOL costume.

Plate of Spaghetti

MATERIALS

- 28" (71 cm) piece of string
- 40" × 40" (101.5 × 101.5 cm) foam core board, ¼" (0.5 cm) thick
- 40" × 10" (101.5 × 25.5 cm) piece of foam core board, ¼" (0.5 cm) thick
- 6 oz (177 mL) red acrylic paint
- 3 oz (90 mL) brown acrylic paint
- 2" (5 cm) wide roll of clear packing tape
- ½" (1.2 cm) wide roll of red tape
- two ½" (1.2 cm) wide rolls of white tape
- two 36" (91.5 cm) pieces of strong red ribbon for straps, 1" (2.5 cm) wide
- red baseball hat
- two 6" (15 cm) diameter Styrofoam balls
- 40' (12 m) polyethylene tubing, ⅜" (1 cm) wide*
- red modeling clay, about a half-pound (224 g)
- four 2" (5 cm) paper clips

*The kind used for fish tank filters

TOOLS: long ruler, pushpin, pencil, pen, craft knife, plastic or rubber glove, sponge (to spread paint), scissors

CHILD WEARS: red sweatshirt, black pants, and black shoes

DIRECTIONS

We will cut two rings out of foam core board. The largest ring will become the outer rim of the plate and the smaller one will become the center of the plate. There will be a space in the center of the plate for the child to stand.

1 Find the center of the 40" × 40" (101.5 × 101.5 cm) foam core board by measuring in 20" (51 cm) on each side. Draw 3 circles—radius 20" (51 cm), radius 13½" (34.3 cm), and radius 7" (18 cm), all with their centers in the center of the foam core board. Use the string, pencil, and pushpin method described on page 53.

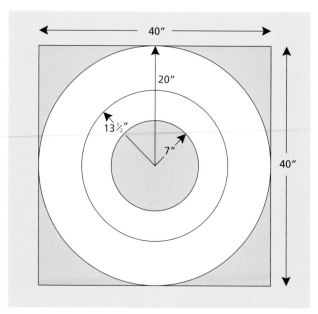

Step 1. Pattern for spaghetti plate. Cut on circles; discard gray parts.

Here's one time your child won't want a second helping.

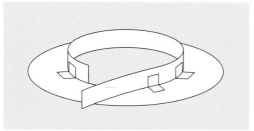

Step 3. Tape the 2" (5 cm) strip of foam core around the inside of the large ring.

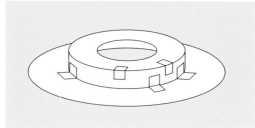

Step 4. Tape the 13½" (34.3 cm) ring onto the strip already in place.

2 Cut along all the circular lines using a craft knife to make rings. Be careful to keep the rings intact as you cut. Discard the 7" (18 cm) radius circle.

3 Cut three 2" × 38" (5 × 96.5 cm) strips of foam core from the 40" × 10" (101.5 × 25.5 cm) foam core board. Tape the ends of the strips together to make one long continuous strip. Break the spine of the foam core by bending the strips into a circle. Tape the strip to the inner circle of the 20" radius (51 cm) ring (see diagram). Cut off any excess strip.

4 Tape the outside of the 13½" (34.3 cm) radius ring to the unattached long edge of the 2" (5 cm) wide foam core strip you just added (see diagram), reinforcing it with 2" (5 cm) wide clear tape. The 13½" ring will become the center of the plate.

5a Turn the assembly you have made upside down, so the lower part is in the center. Tape around the outer edge of the 13½" (34.3 cm) ring with red tape. Tape around the inside circle of the 13½" diameter ring with red tape. Tape around the outer edge of the plate with white tape.

5b To make holes for shoulder straps, poke two holes about 8" (20 cm) apart, about 1" (2.5 cm) out from the inner edge of the red ring, in what will be the front of the costume. Poke two more in what will become the back. Thread a red ribbon through each set of holes in front,

criss-crossing straps, and tie them through the holes in back. Adjust length to your child's height. Pull straps out of the way for Step 6.

6 Wearing a plastic glove, use a sponge to rub red acrylic paint all over the central ring to look like spaghetti sauce. Let dry.

7 Cover both 6" (15 cm) foam balls with red clay to make "meatballs" for your plate. Paint the clay meatballs with brown acrylic paint, letting some of the red show through. Let dry.

8 Partially unbend 2" (5 cm) paper clips, and poke one end up through the bottom of the red foam core ring into each meatball, to secure it.

9 With the child in the red sweatshirt, slip the costume over his head and rest the straps on the shoulders. Cut strips of tubing about 3' (91 cm) long. Twist around the child's body and arms like spaghetti. Don't twist anything around the child's neck.

10 Twist a piece of tubing around the baseball cap and tape in place.

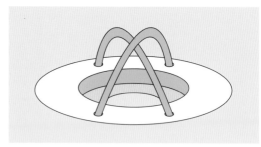

Step 5a and b. The spaghetti plate, turned right-side up, with straps attached.

Speedboat

MATERIALS

- 24" × 48" (61 × 122 cm) piece of corrugated cardboard
- two 7½" × 51" (19 × 129.5 cm) pieces of corrugated cardboard
- 15½" × 18" (39.5 × 46 cm) piece of corrugated cardboard
- 4" × 15" (10 × 38 cm) piece of corrugated cardboard
- 18" × 18" (46 × 46 cm) sheet of red tissue paper
- 28" × 5' (71 × 153 cm) blue wrapping paper
- roll of aluminum foil
- 2" (5 cm) wide clear packing tape
- tacky glue
- ½" (1.2 cm) wide roll of black tape
- acrylic paint: red, white, yellow, and orange
- 3½" × 17" (9 × 43 cm) piece of clear Plexiglas
- twenty-four 3 oz (90 mL) plastic cups
- two pieces of ½" × 24" (1.2 cm × 61 cm) strong black ribbon for straps

TOOLS: ruler, pencil, craft knife, ¼" (0.5 cm) wide paintbrush

CHILD WEARS: orange T-shirt, beach clothes, sandals (or is barefoot)

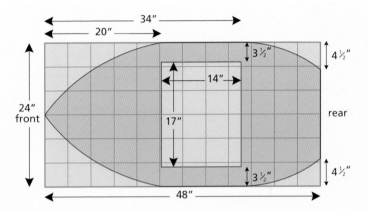

Step 1. Pattern for top of boat. 1 box = 4" (10 cm). Cut away gray parts.

DIRECTIONS

Top of Boat

1 On the 24" × 48" (61 × 122 cm) piece of cardboard, use a pencil to lay out the boat top as shown in the diagram for Step 1, using a ruler for straight lines and drawing the curves freehand.

2 The midpoint on the short side at the left is the front of the boat. The 14" × 17" (35.5 × 43 cm) rectangle in the center of the boat top is the place for the child to stand in while wearing the costume. Cut this rectangle away.

3 Then cut along the sweeping curves to remove the excess cardboard and you will have a piece of cardboard with the general outline of the top of a boat. Set it aside.

Sides and Rear of Boat

4 Lay out the side of the boat as follows:

4a Take one of the 7½" × 51" (19 × 129.5 cm) pieces of cardboard and set it so that one of the long edges is nearest you. Using pencil and a ruler, lay out the side of the boat as shown in the diagram for Step 4. Cut along the curved lines to shape the boat's side.

4b Repeat Step 4a to make the second side in the same way.

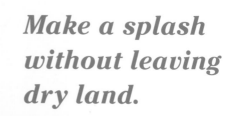

Make a splash without leaving dry land.

Assembly and Finishing

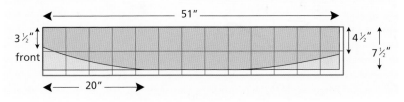

Step 4. Pattern for side of boat. 1 box = 4" (10 cm). Cut away gray parts.

5 Starting from the front point of the boat top, tape each side to the boat top with packing tape. Remember that the long straight edge (51" or 129.5 cm) of the side is the one that should be taped to the boat top. The narrowest (3½" or 9 cm) portion of the boat side should connect to the front of the boat, and the 4½" (11.4 cm) deep portion of the boat side should end up at the rear. Take care to break the spine of the cardboard sides as you go to make it easier to match the curve in the top. Trim any excess off the side at the rear, as needed.

6 The 4" × 15" (10 × 38 cm) piece of cardboard completes the rear portion of the frame. Tape it to both sides in the rear and to the boat top with 2" (5 cm) wide clear packing tape.

7 Cover the entire boat frame with blue wrapping paper, taping it on the inside.

8 Using the 2" (5 cm) wide clear packing tape, attach the piece of Plexiglas to the front of the 14" × 17" (35.5 × 43 cm) opening in which the child will stand. The Plexiglas serves as a windshield. Use black tape around edges of the Plexiglas and in the places that it connects to the blue wrapping paper, to create the appearance of a window frame. You may need to build up the tape on the sides to get the windshield to the desired angle.

9 Mark out the outlines of flames along the boat sides with a pencil; then fill in with the colors of acrylic paint as shown, using one at a time and letting each dry before proceeding (see photo). Let dry.

10 Cut twenty-four 9" × 9" (23 × 23 cm) squares of aluminum foil.

11 Individually wrap each 3 oz (90 mL) plastic cup with an aluminum square.

12 Tacky-glue four cups together, angling each cup up a bit so that you get the appearance of a bent engine pipe (see photo). Repeat this process to make the five other engine pipes. Let dry.

13 Use the 15½" × 18" (39.5 × 46 cm) rectangle of cardboard to cut out an open box that measures 4" × 7½" × 10" (10 × 19 × 25.5 cm) for the engine. Lightly score along the ruling lines and cut away the corners as shown in diagram, but don't fold the box shape yet.

14 Outline and cut out three circular holes on each of the 4" × 10" (10 × 25.5 cm) sides of the engine box, using the bottom of a 3 oz (90 mL) plastic cup as a template; these holes will hold the engine pipes. After cutting the holes, fold the box sides down and tape them together to keep their shape.

15 Cover the engine box in aluminum foil. Tacky-glue a pipe (see Step 12) into each hole. Tear red tissue paper and glue it in the end of each pipe to create the effect of fire coming from the engine pipes.

16 Tape the finished engine box to the top back of the boat with 2" (5 cm) wide clear packing tape.

17 To support the costume, poke one hole into each front and rear corner of the 14" × 17" opening in the top of the boat, a few inches in (5 or 7 cm). Tie the black ribbons through the front holes to create straps to hold the costume on the child. Criss-cross them and tie each off in one of the back corner holes.

Step 13. Pattern for engine box of boat. 1 box = 4" (10 cm). Cut away gray parts; lightly score lines for folding.

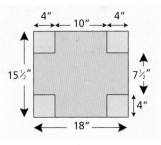

Tic Tac Toe

MATERIALS

- 33" × 34" (84 × 86.4 cm) white foam core board, ½" (1.2 cm) thick
- 11" × 11" (28 × 28 cm) piece of white foam core board, ½" (1.2 cm) thick
- two 1" (2.5 cm) wide rolls of white tape
- four 1" (2.5 cm) wide rolls of red tape
- four 1" (2.5 cm) wide rolls of blue tape
- clear packing tape
- acrylic paints, 3 oz (84 g) of each: white, red, blue, and black
- plastic headband
- 24" (61 cm) curly white ribbon, strong enough for a strap

TOOLS: pencil, long ruler, craft knife, ¼" (0.5 cm) wide paintbrush, scissors, pencil, compass

CHILD WEARS: white shirt, red sweatpants, black shoes

DIRECTIONS

See the diagram to clarify all the measurements discussed below.

1 Orient the foam core board so the 33" (84 cm) side is nearest to you. Rule your 33" × 34" (84 × 86.4 cm) piece of foam core into thirds on its 33" side by marking a line 11" (28 cm) in from the left 34" side and another line 22" (56 cm) in from the same side.

2 By marking an inch (2.5 cm) on either side of the 11" (28 cm) and 22" (56 cm) lines, you will create 2" (5 cm) wide lattice bars for the tic tac toe.

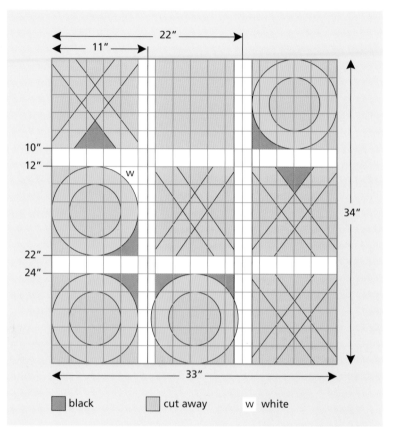

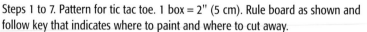

black   cut away   w white

Steps 1 to 7. Pattern for tic tac toe. 1 box = 2" (5 cm). Rule board as shown and follow key that indicates where to paint and where to cut away.

3 From the top, measure down 10" (25.5 cm) on both 34" (86.4 cm) sides and draw a line across the width of the board. Draw another line 2" (5 cm) below it at 12" (30.5 cm) down. Draw another line at 22" (56 cm) down and one at 24" (61 cm) down. These lines mark the horizontal parts of the lattice between the squares.

*What's your
winning strategy?*

4 In four boxes of the lattice (see diagram), draw circles of diameter 10" (25.5 cm). Draw 8½" (21.5 cm) diameter circles inside the 10" ones. Circles must touch or overlap the lattice on 2 or 3 sides so they stay attached. Mark the areas around the "O"s that are to be cut away and the ones to paint black (see diagram). The top central box will be cut away so the child can look out there.

5 On the same cardboard, draw a large "X" in each of 4 remaining boxes (see photo). Each "X" should have sides that are 2½" (6.3 cm) thick and should be the full size of its box.

6 To paint, let each color dry before applying the next. Paint the tic tac toe lattice white. Paint the "O"s red. Paint the "X"s blue. Paint the corners marked black on the diagram black.

7 With a craft knife, carefully cut away the cardboard around the "X"s and "O"s where it is indicated on the diagram to cut, but never cut the letter attachments away from the white lattice.

8 Tape all the cut edges, using tape that matches the color of the letter. Use white tape on the lattice edges.

9 For the headband, draw a 10" (25.5 cm) circle on the 11" × 11" (28 × 28 cm) foam core board. Draw an 8½" (21.5 cm) circle inside it. Cut out the center circle. Paint the "O" red. Let dry. Tape the edges with red tape. Tape the red "O" to the headband with clear tape.

10 Tie white ribbon for a strap around the top bar of the lattice in the center in two places. Hang the tic tac toe sign around the child's neck.

Witch on Broom

MATERIALS

- four 1" × 1" × 16½" (2.5 × 2.5 × 42 cm) pieces of wood
- ten 1" (2.5 cm) drywall screws
- two 2" (5 cm) drywall screws
- 40" long (101.5 cm) small broom
- 5 oz (140 g) bag of purple feathers
- two 8" × 38" (20 × 96.5 cm) strips of striped fabric for legs
- small size 6 children's tennis shoes (thrift store)
- 10 oz (280 g) bag polyester batting
- 20" × 72" (51 × 183 cm) black fabric
- 17" × 40" (43 × 101.5 cm) black fabric
- 40" (101.5 cm) black ribbon, ½" (1.2 cm) wide
- 50" (127 cm) black ribbon, ½" (1.2 cm) wide
- witch's hat

TOOLS: screwdriver, drill, hot glue gun, scissors, needle and thread, saw, staple gun

CHILD WEARS: purple long-sleeved top, black shorts or skirt, white tights, and black shoes

DIRECTIONS

1 Use the four pieces of wood to create a rectangular frame by joining the pieces of wood together at their ends with 1" (2.5 cm) drywall screws. Use two drywall screws at each corner.

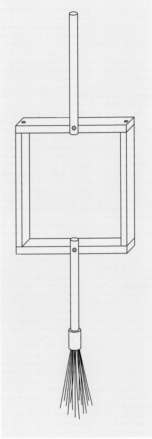

Steps 1 to 3. Assemble frame as shown and attach 2 pieces of broomstick.

2 Cut off the top 16" (41 cm) of the broomstick with a saw.

3 Mark the midpoint of one side of the frame. Drill a hole through the frame at the midpoint for a 2" (5 cm) drywall screw. Place one end of the 16" length of broomstick flush behind the wood frame, centering it on the tip of the drill, and drill through the broomstick also. Attach the 16" broomstick piece to the frame with a 2" (5 cm) drywall screw. On the opposite side of the frame, attach the remaining, lower portion of the broomstick in the same way. There is no broomstick inside the frame, leaving room for the child to stand.

4 To make the witch's legs, fold each of the 8" × 38" (20 × 96.5 cm) pieces of striped fabric in half to 4" × 38" (10 × 96.5 cm), with right sides of fabric facing in. Sew the long sides closed with needle and thread. Stitch one short end closed also. Repeat for the second piece of striped fabric.

5 Turn the leg right-side out and fill solidly with batting.

6 On the sides of the wooden frame that don't have any broomstick attached, attach a small tennis shoe on the outside of frame, close to the bristly end of the broom (see photo), by screwing it into the frame with a 1" (2.5 cm) screw.

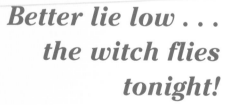

Better lie low . . . the witch flies tonight!

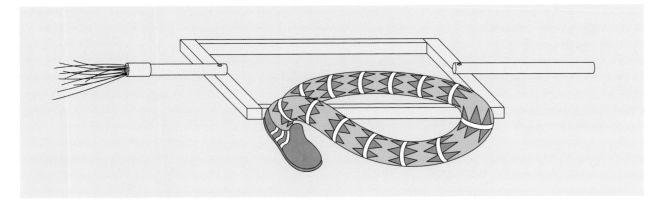

Steps 6 and 7. After sneaker is nailed to frame, stuffed leg is bent, part is inserted in sneaker, and the leg is stapled onto the frame in 2 places.

7 Stick the closed end of the batting-filled leg into the hole in the shoe to act as a foot. Align the leg on the side of the frame and staple it to the side of the frame near the front. Bend the rest of the leg back over the shoe and staple the leg to the top of the wooden frame. Repeat this on the opposite side of the frame with the second leg.

8 To make the skirt, fold the 20" × 72" (51 × 183 cm) black fabric in 1" (2.5 cm) on one side to make a 19" × 72" (48 × 183 cm) piece with a 1" hem. Sew down the hem near its edge to make a 1" tube for the ribbon.

9 Slip the 50" × ½" (127 × 1.2 cm) ribbon through the tube, gathering the fabric of the skirt as you go, until the ribbon has been fed all the way through. Leave excess ribbon to tie the skirt onto the child, around the waist.

10 Wrap the black skirt around the outside of frame, folding it back to leave the legs and shoes exposed. Bring a little of the fabric under and inside the frame and staple it on the inside of the frame. The skirt should hang approximately 14" (35 cm) from waist to bottom of frame.

11 Take the witch's hat and hot-glue purple feathers around the top brim of the hat.

12 To make the cape, fold the 17" × 40" (43 × 101.5 cm) piece of black fabric to make a 14" × 40" (35.5 × 101.5 cm) shape with a 3" (7.5 cm) hem. Then fold over another 3½" (9 cm) to make an 11½" × 40" (20 × 101.5 cm) shape.

13 Sew across the cape fabric ½" (1.2 cm) in from the last fold, all the way across the 40" (101.5 cm) width to make a ½" (1.2 cm) wide tube to thread the ½" × 40" ribbon through, leaving you with a cape with a collar.

14 After the child is dressed, tie the costume on around her waist and tie the cape around her neck.

Lollipops and Sugar Sticks

MATERIALS

- three pieces of ¾" × 12" (1.9 × 30.5 cm) PVC pipe (for uprights)
- two pieces of ¾" × 18" (1.9 × 45.5 cm) PVC pipe (sides)
- two pieces of ¾" × 36" (1.9 × 91.5 cm) PVC pipe (for lollipop sticks)
- ¾" × 22" (1.9 × 56 cm) PVC pipe (for lollipop stick)
- ¾" × 9" (1.9 × 23 cm) PVC pipe
- seven pieces of ¾" × 2½" (1.9 × 6.4 cm) PVC pipe
- four ¾" (1.9 cm) PVC elbows: 3 regular elbows and 1 side outlet elbow*
- six ¾" (1.9 cm) PVC straight-through T connectors
- PVC pipe glue
- 2" (5 cm) wide red tape
- 2" (5 cm) wide clear packing tape
- four 15" (38 cm) diameter disposable see-through dish covers, the kind used for catering (for large lollipops)
- two 12" (30.5 cm) diameter disposable see-through dish covers (for small lollipop)
- five round 5" (12.5 cm) diameter see-through disposable containers (for round candies)
- acrylic paint, 6 oz (177 mL): white, hot pink, orange, yellow, and red
- plastic headband
- two pieces of 40" (102 cm) white ribbon for straps, 1" (2.5 cm) wide
- two 12" × 18" (30.5 × 45.5 cm) sheets of shiny hot pink wrapping paper
- three 12" × 18" (30.5 × 45.5) sheets of shiny deep purple wrapping paper
- 10' (300 cm) purple ribbon, ½" (1.2 cm) wide
- 10' (300 cm) hot pink ribbon, ½" (1.2 cm) wide
- 10' (300 cm) ribbon, ¼" (6 mm) wide, in each of the following: green, red, pink, blue, light green, yellow
- one each of 2" (5 cm) wide cardboard tubes, wrapped in white butcher paper, in the following lengths: 18" (45.5 cm), 12½" (32 cm), 17" (43 cm), 23" (58.4 cm)**
- two 2" wide × 17½" (5 × 44.5 cm) cardboard tubes wrapped in green wrapping paper**
- one each of 1½" (3.8 cm) wide cardboard tubes wrapped in green paper, in the following lengths: 11" (28 cm), 12" (30.5 cm)**
- one each of 1½" (3.8 cm) wide cardboard tubes, wrapped in yellow wrapping paper, in the following lengths: 14" (35.5 cm), 22" (56 cm), 23" (58.4 cm), 13" (33 cm)**
- ½" (1.2 cm) wide × 8" (20 cm) cardboard tube (e.g., fax paper roll) covered in white butcher paper (for hairband)**
- tacky glue

*The side outlet elbow has an extra hole at the top for a pipe.
**Before starting the steps below, wrap each cardboard tube neatly in paper and tape the paper ends inside the tube.

TOOLS: scissors, paintbrushes, ruler, craft knife

CHILD WEARS: solid bright colors and white shoes, or just socks

DIRECTIONS

Basically, you will assemble a frame from PVC components that is about 20" (51 cm) deep and 21" (53.3 cm) wide. The lollipops (suckers), round candies, and candy sticks all will be

*Life is sweeter
with a little
extra sugar.*

attached to this frame. The child will stand inside the frame. There are some extra decorations on the headband. We give you the basic instructions, but improvise as you see fit. Unless otherwise noted, all taping is done with clear tape. Gluing of PVC parts to each other should be done with PVC pipe glue.

Candies

1 Take all wrapped cardboard tubes and wind them with ribbons of different colors and thicknesses: Tape one end of each ribbon using 2" (5 cm) clear packing tape and twist ribbon around the tube to create a spiral pattern, cutting and taping the ribbon's end at the other end of the tube. Use any ribbons or combination of ribbons that look good to you.

2 To make the round wrapped candies, wrap each of three plastic 5" (12.5) circular containers in a 12" × 18" (20.5 × 45.5 cm) sheet of shiny deep purple wrapping paper. Twist ends of wrapping paper so the containers look like wrapped candies (see photo); tie each end closed with ribbon.

3 Repeat Step 2 for two more containers, but use shiny hot pink wrapping paper instead. Set them aside.

4 Lollipops: Paint a spiral onto the inside of both halves of each of the large (15" or 38 cm) diameter) plastic dish covers, using a bright color of acrylic paint. After the spirals you have painted have dried, coat the entire inside of the container with either a darker or lighter color of acrylic paint. You could use a red spiral with a solid white background or an orange spiral with a yellow background, for example. Do the same for the 12" (30.5 cm) diameter see-through dish covers, which will become the smaller lollipop. Use your imagination and have fun. There are two sides to every lollipop, so

paint these in pairs, using the same color scheme. Let the covers dry. From the outside, you will see the original spiral; the rest of the cover will appear to be filled with the second color. Glue the two matching lollipop sides together. For each lollipop, cut a small hole in the seam to hold a ¾" (1.9 cm) PVC pipe section (the lollipop stick). Set these parts aside.

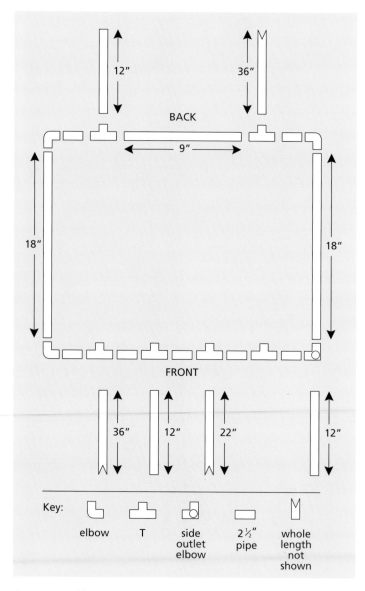

Step 5. Assembly diagram for PVC frame. Turn T connectors and side outlet elbow so openings are facing up.

Frame for Costume

5 Follow the Step 5 diagram to lay out the frame for the costume, but don't glue the pieces together yet:

5a On a flat work surface, connect a PVC elbow to each end of an 18" (45.5 cm) pipe; this will become the side of the frame on your left.

5b To make the back of the frame, working from your left to right, attach a 2½" (6.4 cm) piece of pipe, a T connector, a 9" (23 cm) piece of pipe, another T connector, another 2½" piece of pipe, and finally another elbow.

5c For the side of the frame on your right, add an 18" (45.5 cm) PVC pipe to the elbow at the back, and then add a side outlet elbow at the front. (The side outlet elbow has an extra hole for an upright.)

5d To make the front, connect all 5 remaining 2½" (6.4 cm) pipes between the remaining 4 T connectors (see diagram).

5e Attach the assembled front piece to the sides of the frame, at the elbows. With the frame flat on your work surface, rotate your T connectors so that all the open holes on the connectors are facing straight up.

5f Slide the 17½" (44.5 cm) green cardboard tubes over the two 18" (45.5 cm) pipes that make up the sides of the frame; you must temporarily disconnect the pipes to do this.

5g Once you have gotten the frame pieces well aligned, disconnect, glue, and reconnect each piece and connector, one at a time. Make sure to wait the amount of drying time specified on the PVC glue before moving to the next connector, and be careful to maintain alignment as you go.

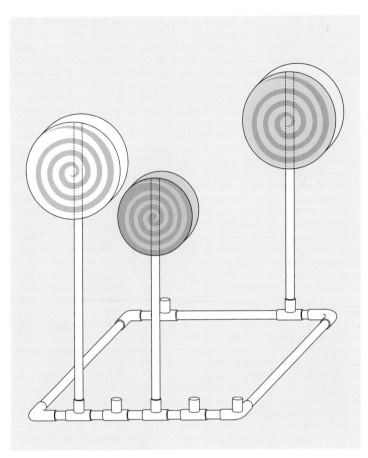

Step 7. Partially assembled frame, showing lollipops in place.

6 While you are facing the front of the frame, insert two 12" (30.5 cm) PVC pipes in the T connector and the side outlet elbow on the front of the frame (see diagram for Step 5) and one 12" pipe in the T connector on the left rear of the frame. All inserted pipes should be upright (vertical). Once you have them in position, disconnect, glue, and reconnect.

7 Twist ribbon around the two 36" (91.5 cm) PVC pipes and insert one pipe into a T connector in the back to your right and one in the front at your left. Disconnect, glue, and reconnect. These are the sticks for the large lollipops.

8 On the front of the frame, starting from the 12" pipe at your right front:

8a Slip the 2" diameter × 18" (5 × 45.5 cm) white cardboard tube over the 12" (30.5 cm) upright pipe (in the elbow).

8b On the first T connector from the right, tape the 2" × 12½" white cardboard tube with clear tape, holding it at an angle (see photo). This cardboard tube is taped directly onto the T connector.

8c Slip the 1½" diameter × 22" (3.8 × 56 cm) yellow cardboard tube over the upright pipe in the second T connector from the right.

8d The 1½" diameter × 12" (3.8 × 30.5 cm) green cardboard tube goes over the upright PVC pipe in the third T connector from the right.

8e The large lollipop top (15" or 38 cm diameter) gets attached to the 36" (91.5 cm) PVC pipe in the fourth T connector from the right. Insert the unattached 36" pipe end through the hole in the center seam of the lollipop top and push the top down as far as it will go. Then tape the top in place with clear tape.

8f Glue and tape the 12" (30.5 cm) diameter lollipop top to the 22" (56 cm) piece of PVC pipe in the second T connector from the right.

9 Facing the front of the costume and starting on your right in the front, tape the 1½" × 11" (3.8 × 28 cm) green cardboard tube, the 1½" × 14" (3.8 × 35.5 cm) yellow cardboard tube, and the 2" × 23" (5 × 58.4 cm) white cardboard tube in a bunch to the 2" × 18" white cardboard tube

in the right front elbow. Tape a hot pink round candy (see Step 3) to the frame in front of those tubes you just attached.

10 Tape the 2" × 17" (5 × 43 cm) white tube horizontally along the front left part of the frame (as you face it), below the upright pipes (see photo).

11 Tape a round purple candy (from Step 2) above the white tube you just attached to the frame, and tape one in front of the smaller lollipop.

12 Tape a hot pink candy to the front of the green post between the two purple candies you just attached.

13 Cover the 12" (30.5 cm) upright pipe at your left at the back of the costume with the 1½" diameter × 23" (3.8 × 58.4 cm) yellow cardboard tube.

14 Tape and glue a 15" (38 cm) diameter lollipop to the top of the 36" (91 cm) tall PVC pipe at the back on your right. Set the costume aside.

15 Cover the headband in red tape. With clear packing tape, tape the 1½" × 13" (2.5 × 33 cm) yellow cardboard tube to the headband. On top of the yellow tube, tape the ½" (1.2 cm) × 8" (20 cm) white cardboard tube. Tape a round purple candy on top of the tubes on the headband.

16 Have the child stand in the costume, holding it at about hip height. Tie the white ribbons on the front frame corners, criss-cross them behind her shoulders, and tie the other ends on the frame corners at the rear to support the costume.

About the Author

Growing up in Burbank, California, Holly Cleeland was exposed to the art of costume at an early age. The youngest of five children, she frequently accompanied her mother, Arden Cleeland, a costumer for many famous movie and television stars, to the stars' homes and movie sets. In this way, she met famous actresses including Elsa Lanchester, Susan St. James, Nancy Walker, and Stella Stevens. As a child of 4, Holly got to see a dragon for Disneyland being built in her own front room.

Being around creative activities and creative people inspired her in all areas. With such role models, it wasn't long before Holly started making costumes for family members and neighborhood friends, sharing in their delight when her creations won prizes.

During her high school years, Holly made money by painting T-shirts, designing store windows at holiday time, and drawing portraits, among other things. After attending Los Angeles Trade Tech and the Pasadena Art Center, in 1988 Holly started creating and selling Lawn Cheers, outdoor lawn displays for the holidays, an activity that takes her to many large art shows up and down the California coast. She also markets Lawn Cheers through many mail order catalogs. Her unique and easy-to-make costumes and lawn decorations have been featured on "The Rosie O'Donnell Show" and on HGTV's "The Carol Duvall Show." Holly lives in North Hollywood with her cat, Pumpkin.

Index